Mastering
Primary
Religious
Education

Edited by Judith Roden and James Archer

The *Mastering Primary Teaching* series provides an insight into the core principles underpinning each of the subjects of the Primary National Curriculum, thereby helping student teachers to 'master' the subjects. This in turn will enable new teachers to share this mastery in their teaching. Each book follows the same sequence of chapters, which has been specifically designed to assist trainee teachers to capitalize on opportunities to develop pedagogical excellence. These comprehensive guides introduce the subject and help trainees know how to plan and teach effective and inspiring lessons that make learning irresistible. Examples of children's work and case studies are included to help exemplify what is considered to be the best and most innovative practice in primary education. The series is written by leading professionals, who draw on their years of experience to provide authoritative guides to the primary curriculum subject areas.

Also available in the series

Mastering Primary English, Wendy Jolliffe and David Waugh

Mastering Primary Languages, Paula Ambrossi and Darnelle Constant-Shepherd

Mastering Primary Geography, Anthony Barlow and Sarah Whitehouse

Mastering Primary Music, Ruth Atkinson

Mastering Primary Physical Education, Kristy Howells with Alison Carney, Neil Castle and Rich Little

Mastering Primary Science, Amanda McCrory and Kenna Worthington

Forthcoming in the series

Mastering Primary Art and Design, Peter Gregory, Claire March and Suzy Tutchell

Mastering Primary Computing, Graham Parton and Christine Kemp-Hall

Mastering Primary Design and Technology, Gill Hope

Mastering Primary History, Karin Doull, Christopher Russell and Alison Hales

Mastering Primary Mathematics, Andrew Lamb, Rebecca Heaton and Helen Taylor

Also available from Bloomsbury

Developing Teacher Expertise, edited by Margaret Sangster

Readings for Reflective Teaching in Schools, edited by Andrew Pollard

Reflective Teaching in Schools, Andrew Pollard

Mastering Primary Religious Education

Maria James and Julian Stern

BLOOMSBURY ACADEMIC
LONDON · NEW YORK · OXFORD · NEW DELHI · SYDNEY

BLOOMSBURY ACADEMIC
Bloomsbury Publishing Plc
50 Bedford Square, London, WC1B 3DP, UK
1385 Broadway, New York, NY 10018, USA

BLOOMSBURY, BLOOMSBURY ACADEMIC and the Diana logo are trademarks of
Bloomsbury Publishing Plc

First published in Great Britain 2019

Cover design: Anna Berzovan
Cover image © iStock (miakievy / molotovcoketail)

A catalogue record for this book is available from the British Library.

A catalog record for this book is available from the Library of Congress.

ISBN: HB: 978-1-4742-9697-7
PB: 978-1-4742-9698-4
ePDF: 978-1-4742-9699-1
eBook: 978-1-4742-9700-4

Series: Mastering Primary Teaching

Typeset by Deanta Global Publishing Services, Chennai, India
Printed and bound in Great Britain

To find out more about our authors and books visit www.bloomsbury.com
and sign up for our newsletters.

Contents

About the Authors

Julian Stern is Professor of Education and Religion at York St John University. He was a school teacher for fourteen years, and has worked in universities for twenty-five years. Julian is widely published, with fifteen books and over thirty articles, including *A Philosophy of Schooling: Care and Curiosity in Community* (2018), *Teaching Religious Education: Researchers in the Classroom: Second Edition* (2018), *Can I Tell You About Loneliness* (2017), *Virtuous Educational Research: Conversations on Ethical Practice* (2016), *Loneliness and Solitude in Schools: How to Value Individuality and Create an Enstatic School* (2014), *The Spirit of the School* (2009), *Schools and Religions: Imagining the Real* (2007) and *Involving Parents* (2003).

Figure 0.1 Julian Stern, by Shauna Lang (aged nine)

Maria James is a principal lecturer. She teaches RE and masters programmes, and is Programme Director for Masters in Academic Practice at St Mary's University. She works within initial teacher education with responsibility for primary RE and  co-convenes the Masters in Education programme. Maria has worked in the field of education for over forty years, first as a primary school teacher with responsibility for art and RE for some twenty years, and secondly within university-based teacher education at Brunel University, Roehampton University and St Mary's University. She was a founding member of her local SACRE in Kingston upon Thames and has been Chair for the last twelve years. She is Vice Chair of the professional Association of University Lecturers in Religion and Education (AULRE). She has presented and published several papers about RE and her doctoral thesis was about faith and values-based practice.

Figure 0.2 Maria James, by Esther Grace Herring (aged eight)

List of Figures

Series Editors' Foreword

A long and varied experience of working with beginner and experienced teachers in primary schools has informed this series since its conception. Over the last thirty years there have been many changes in practice in terms of teaching and learning in primary and early years education. Significantly, since the implementation of the first National Curriculum in 1989 the aim has been to bring best practice in primary education to all state schools in England and Wales. As time has passed, numerous policy decisions have altered the detail and emphasis of the delivery of the primary curriculum. However, there has been little change in the belief that pupils in the primary and early years phases of education should receive a broad, balanced curriculum based on traditional subjects.

Recent Ofsted subject reports and notably the Cambridge Primary Review indicate that rather than the ideal being attained, in many schools, the emphasis on English and mathematics has not only depressed the other subjects of the primary curriculum, but also narrowed the range of strategies used for the delivery of the curriculum. The amount of time allocated to subject sessions in initial teacher education courses has dramatically reduced, which may also account for this narrow diet in pedagogy.

The vision for this series of books was borne out of our many years of experience with student teachers. As a result, we believe that the series is well designed to equip trainee and beginner teachers to master the art of teaching in the primary phase. This series of books aims to introduce current and contemporary practices associated with the whole range of subjects within the Primary National Curriculum and religious education. It also goes beyond this by providing beginner teachers with the knowledge and understanding required to achieve mastery of each subject. In doing so, each book in the series highlights contemporary issues such as assessment and inclusion which are the key areas that even the most seasoned practitioner is still grappling with in light of the introduction of the new Primary Curriculum. In agreement with the results attached with these books, we believe that students who work in schools and progress onto their Newly Qualified Teacher year will be able to make a significant contribution to the provision in their school, especially in foundation subjects.

Readers will find great support within each one of these books. Each book in the series will inform and provide the opportunity for basic mastery of each of the subjects, namely English, mathematics, science, physical education, music, history, geography, design and technology, computing and religious education. They will discover the essence of each subject in terms of its philosophy, knowledge and skills. Readers will also be inspired by the enthusiasm for each subject revealed by the subject authors who are experts in their field. They will discover many and varied strategies for making each subject 'come alive' for their pupils and they should become more confident about teaching across the whole range of subjects represented in the primary and early years curriculum.

Primary teaching in the state sector is characterized by a long history of pupils being taught the whole range of the primary curriculum by one teacher. Although some schools may employ specialists to deliver some subjects of the curriculum, notably physical education, music or science, for example, it is more usual for the whole curriculum to be delivered to a class by their class teacher. This places a potentially enormous burden on beginner teachers no matter which route they enter teaching. The burden is especially high on those entering through employment-based routes and for those who aim to become inspiring primary teachers. There is much to learn!

The term 'mastery' is generally considered to relate to knowledge and understanding of a subject which incorporates the 'how' of teaching as well as the 'what'. Although most entrants to primary teaching will have some experience of the primary curriculum as a pupil, very few will have experienced the breadth of the curriculum or may have any understanding of the curriculum which reflects recent trends in teaching and learning within the subject. The primary curriculum encompasses a very broad range of subjects, each of which has its own knowledge base, skills and ways of working. Unsurprisingly, very few new entrants into the teaching profession hold mastery of all the interrelated subjects. Indeed for the beginner teacher it may well be many years before full mastery of all aspects of the primary curriculum is achieved. The content of the primary curriculum has changed significantly, notably in some foundation subjects, such as history and music. So although beginner teachers might hold fond memories of these subjects from their own experience of primary education, the content of the subject may well have changed significantly over time and may incorporate different emphases.

This series, Mastering Primary Teaching, aims to meet the needs of those who, reflecting the desire for mastery over each subject, want to know more. This is a tall order. Nevertheless, we believe that the pursuit of development should always be rewarded, which is why we are delighted to have so many experts sharing their well-developed knowledge and passion for the subjects featured in each book. The vision for this series is to provide support for those who are beginning their teaching career, who may not feel fully secure in their subject knowledge, understanding and skill.

In addition, the series also aims to provide a reference point for beginner teachers to always be able to go back to support them in the important art of teaching.

Intending primary teachers, in our experience, have a thirst for knowledge about the subject that they will be teaching. They want to 'master' new material and ideas in a range of subjects. They aim to gain as much knowledge as they can of the subjects they will be teaching, in some of which the beginner teachers may lack in confidence or may be scared of because of their perceived lack of familiarity with some subjects and particularly how they are delivered in primary schools. Teaching the primary curriculum can be one of the most rewarding experiences. We believe that this series will help the beginner teachers to unlock the primary curriculum in a way that ensures they establish themselves as confident primary practitioners.

Judith Roden
James Archer
June 2017

How to Use This Book

This book is one of twelve books that together help form a truly innovative series that is aimed to support your development. Each book follows the same format and chapter sequence. There is an emphasis throughout the book on providing information about the teaching and learning of religious education. You will find a wealth of information within each chapter that will help you to understand the issues, problems and opportunities that teaching the subject can provide you as a developing practitioner in the subject. Crucially, each chapter provides opportunities for you to reflect upon important points linked to your development in order that you may master the teaching of religious education. As a result you will develop your confidence in the teaching of a primary religious education. There really is something for everyone within each chapter.

Each chapter has been carefully designed to help you to develop your knowledge of the subject systematically and as a result contains key features. Chapter objectives clearly signpost the content of each chapter and these will help you to familiarize yourself with important aspects of the subject and will orientate you in preparation for reading the chapter. The regular 'Pause for thought' points offer questions and activities for you to reflect on important aspects of the subject. Each 'Pause for thought' provides you with an opportunity to enhance your learning beyond merely reading the chapter. These will sometimes ask you to consider your own experience and what you already know about the teaching of the subject. Others will require you to critique aspects of good practice presented as case studies or research. To benefit fully from reading this text, you need to be an active participant. Sometimes you are asked to make notes on your response to questions and ideas and then to revisit these later on in your reading. While it would be possible for you to skip through the opportunities for reflection or to give only cursory attention to the questions and activities which aim to facilitate deeper reflection than might otherwise be the case, we strongly urge you to engage with the 'Pause for thought' activities. It is our belief that it is through these moments that most of your transformational learning will occur as a result of engaging this book. At the end of each chapter, you will find a summary of main points from the chapter along with suggestions for further reading.

We passionately believe that learners of all ages learn best when they work with others, so we would encourage you, if possible, to work with another person, sharing your ideas and perspectives. The book also would be ideal for group study within a university or school setting.

This book has been authored by Maria James and Julian Stern, who are experienced and highly regarded as professionals in their subject area. They are strong voices within the primary religious education community. By reading this book you will be able to benefit from their rich knowledge, understanding and experience. When using this ensure that you are ready to learn from some of the greats in primary religious education.

Acknowledgements

The authors would like to thank all those who contributed to this project, especially the pupils, student teachers, teachers, university colleagues and NATRE (http://www.natre.org.uk and its RE advisor Lat Blaylock), who provided examples of their work.

Chapter 1
An Introduction to Primary Religious Education

Chapter objectives

- What is primary religious education (RE) and why should it be on the curriculum?
- Some aims of RE
- What does it mean for pupils to become religiously literate?
- How can RE contribute to a child's whole development?

Introduction

To start at the beginning, welcome to *Mastering Primary Religious Education*. You are probably reading this book because you are learning to be a primary school teacher who will be required to teach RE or you may be a teacher from a variety of settings who wants to investigate the subject further. This book aims to help you develop critical understanding of the importance, purpose and relevance of effective RE in the primary curriculum. The text seeks to examine concepts and themes within RE and how these might be investigated and developed. In considering the art of teaching the subject and through exploring different pedagogies and conceptual frameworks, it is hoped that you will discover how the subject has at its heart the aim of nurturing confident, religiously literate citizens. Such pupils are increasingly aware of the positive contribution that they can make to their society while being respectful and appreciative of beliefs and cultures that are different to their own. In short, in learning through effective RE, pupils can develop more as critical human beings who can think for themselves, which is, after all, the ultimate purpose of all good education.

This chapter introduces you to the irresistible subject of RE for the primary classroom. Some of the main aims are considered as you get to know the subject. There are various tasks for you to complete throughout this chapter and those that follow, and it would be beneficial for you to keep a reflective notebook close by, so that

Figure 1.1 Creation, by pupils from St Mary and St Thomas Aquinas Catholic Primary School, Gateshead

you can note anything of significance as your knowledge and understanding of RE develops and as you grow as a reflective teacher of the subject. In addition, you will consider how you might develop religious literacy with your pupils and start to think about planning effective RE (Figure 1.1).

What is primary religious education (RE) and why should it be on the curriculum?

This first chapter introduces you to what RE is and why it is an important part of the primary curriculum. So, there are a few things you need to know. We begin with what one Secretary of State for Education had to say:

> All children need to acquire core knowledge and understandings of the beliefs and practices of the religions and worldviews which not only shape their history and culture but which guide their own development. The modern world needs young people who are sufficiently confident in their own beliefs and values that they can respect the religious and cultural differences of others, and contribute to a cohesive and compassionate society.
>
> Michael Gove, in his foreword to REC 2013b, p 5

Figure 1.2 Our journey of faith, by pupils from St Mary and St Thomas Aquinas Catholic Primary School, Gateshead

RE is a subject with a unique, distinctive contribution to make to the curriculum, drawing on the cultures and histories of the world's traditions, and on the personal experiences of the pupils in the classroom. It should be 'academically challenging and personally inspiring' (REC 2013b, p 7). So, in RE, pupils gain knowledge and understanding of the way people make sense of the world through religion and belief. These religions and beliefs are expressed in many ways, through writings, art, architecture, music, ritual and action. In effective RE pupils can come to an appreciation of the diversity of such expression and participate in dialogue about these in their society. Through starting to consider and develop their own ideas about how they make sense of their lives and the world in which they live, they develop as citizens of the world. So, look at the way these pupils chart their journey of faith (Figure 1.2).

RE can help pupils 'consider challenging questions of meaning, purpose, truth, values and commitments, and the answers offered by religions and non-religious worldviews' (Pett 2015, p 2). The RE Council puts it this way:

> Religious education contributes dynamically to children's and young people's education in schools by provoking challenging questions about meaning and purpose in life, beliefs about God, ultimate reality, issues of right and wrong and what it means to be human.
>
> REC 2013a, p 14

RE is a statutory subject in primary schools, supported by non-statutory guidance and, for many schools, a statutory locally Agreed Syllabus. The National Curriculum document (DfE 2013) stipulates that all state schools must teach RE and must publish their curriculum by subject and academic year online. Schools with a religious foundation will follow their diocesan guidelines or syllabuses composed according to guidance from faith organizations. The subject is not, in primary schools, called Religious Instruction or Religious Studies but Religious Education. In RE, pupils can learn about and from Christianity and the principal religious traditions represented in Great Britain (DES 1988), considered to be Buddhism, Hinduism, Islam, Judaism and Sikhism, while they develop and start to make sense of their own beliefs and views that help give meaning to their lives. They also explore non-religious worldviews. The subject has a unique contribution to make to community cohesion and citizenship by its mandate to develop knowledge and understanding of the different religions and secular worldviews that form part of the contemporary culture of a multi-faith society.

Pause for thought

Would you recognize the six symbols for Christianity and the other principal religions represented in Great Britain? How could you use the symbols to introduce your teaching about the religions? You may also like to find out about the Happy Human symbol and what it represents (see https://humanism.org.uk). Using this symbol, young children might consider what makes people happy and how sad people can be supported. What symbol would children design for what they believe?

RE is part of the basic curriculum, and although it is not described or prescribed in the National Curriculum (DfE 2013), it follows the National Curriculum's remit for every state-funded school to provide a balanced and broadly based curriculum that

- promotes the spiritual, moral, cultural, mental and physical development of pupils;
- prepares pupils at the school for the opportunities, responsibilities and experiences of later life.

(DfE 2013, p 4)

In this book, you will find a number of tasks that will help you engage with the subject more thoroughly. The plan is that through completing the tasks and engaging with suggested wider reading about the subject, you will develop and extend your pedagogical knowledge and further enhance your skill and art to teach the irresistible subject of RE with flair and confidence. That is why we have suggested keeping a notebook near to write down insights from the suggested readings and anything else that develops your thinking. You might like to use the following:

- What I did (I read, watched, spoke to a teacher in school, taught, etc.).
- What I learned.
- The significance of my learning for my development as an RE teacher.

Take your time over the tasks in this chapter, as you begin to consider the subject and yourself as an RE teacher. Take time to dwell. You might like to revisit some of the tasks as you continue through the rest of the book and as your experience of teaching RE develops.

Some aims of RE

To understand more about the value of RE, we begin by considering the main aims of the subject. There are numerous aims offered in all the documents associated with RE and sometimes this can be overwhelming. Like values, such aims can appear as abstract, until worked through in practice. It calls on the art of the teacher to take these aims and work with them for the benefit of pupils' development. The aims need to be realized in schemes of study with effective modes of learning, so the school's RE coordinator will need to collaborate with colleagues to plan effective RE, but you can engage with some of these here.

Task one: What does effective RE aim to do?

Look at the following grid. Decide which five aims you would list for the subject and two that you would discard. You might like to add a couple of your own if you think they are not included. Give reasons for your choices.

To help pupils understand some of the main ideas that have shaped the world and civilization as we know it	To make sure pupils have knowledge of the Bible	To develop certain concepts, attitudes, skills and knowledge through studying religions and worldviews	To explore those aspects of human experience that help people make sense of life and living
To develop knowledge and understanding of Buddhism, Christianity, Hinduism, Islam, Judaism and Sikhism	To teach pupils about Christianity as a part of the UK's history and heritage	To help pupils make decisions about which faith to adopt – to give them a choice	To help pupils learn more about their own religious or non-religious tradition and heritage

To nurture pupils' spiritual development	To develop an understanding of the variety of ways in which religious belief can be expressed, for example, through music and art	To develop pupils' ability to think about questions of belief and value	To provide a framework to allow pupils to learn about the complex nature of society and how religions contribute to it
To explore a range of questions responding to human experience and to consider ways in which religions and non-religious worldviews respond to ultimate questions	To help pupils understand what it means to hold a religious view of life through understanding the main beliefs and practices of the main religions	To promote tolerance and sensitivity towards those with beliefs different from one's own	To teach pupils how to behave and make moral choices about how to act and live
To help pupils understand and respect different viewpoints and perspectives	To prepare pupils for life where they will meet people from different religious and non-religious traditions	To help pupils to develop religious literacy	To develop skills of enquiry, analysis and evaluation to help pupils make connections between the beliefs of others with how they, themselves, make sense of their world

The writers of the non-statutory framework for RE (REC 2013b) list the following aims. These are not statutory, and they are not quite the same as the aims listed in the previous activity, or in the syllabuses your schools may follow. They are included in full here as they offer a good example of an approach to RE focused on gaining knowledge and understanding and developing religious literacy.

The curriculum for RE aims to ensure that all pupils:

A   Know about and understand a range of religions and worldviews, so that they can

   ● describe, explain and analyse beliefs and practices, recognising the diversity which exists within and between communities and amongst individuals;

- identify, investigate and respond to questions posed, and responses offered by some of the sources of wisdom found in religions and world views;
- appreciate and appraise the nature, significance and impact of different ways of life and ways of expressing meaning.

B Express ideas and insights about the nature, significance and impact of religions and worldviews, so that they can

- explain reasonably their ideas about how beliefs, practices and forms of expression influence individuals and communities;
- express with increasing discernment their personal reflections and critical responses to questions and teachings about identity, diversity, meaning and value, including ethical issues;
- appreciate and appraise varied dimensions of religion or a worldview

C Gain and deploy the skills needed to engage seriously with religions and worldviews, so that they can

- find out about and investigate key concepts and questions of belonging, meaning, purpose and truth, responding creatively;
- enquire into what enables different individuals and communities to live together respectfully for the wellbeing of all;
- articulate beliefs, values and commitments clearly in order to explain why they may be important in their own and other people's lives.

(REC 2013b, pp 14–15)

It is worthwhile highlighting some of the action verbs that are included in the above (these are imperatives and some pupils call them 'bossy verbs'), and think about what could be done in RE to achieve *four* of these aims.

What does it mean for pupils to become religiously literate?

One underlying purpose that runs throughout the list offered by the RE Council and others (although the phrase is implied rather than explicitly used) is that pupils might become religiously literate. Religious literacy has its roots and genesis in concerns about the current lack of knowledge of basic ideas and narratives, and the difficulty people have in discussing religious issues. Often, in the many popular quiz programmes that exist, there is an acceptance of not knowing when it comes to questions about religion. This common acceptance of ignorance is curious given the important part that religion has played and continues to play in this country, and in the formation of civilization as we know it. You might like to think about traces of religion evidenced in this country's architecture, art, fiction, society and culture. Being religiously literate includes and goes beyond the ability to recall facts and figures about religion (where Makkah is situated or identifying the third commandment), and it cannot be assumed that those who hold a religious faith or worldview with conviction (and it could be argued that includes everyone) are necessarily religiously literate. Pupils can develop the skills of being religiously literate through

- **investigating** religions and worldviews through varied experiences, approaches and disciplines;
- **reflecting on** and **expressing** their own ideas and the ideas of others with increasing creativity and clarity;
- becoming increasingly **able to respond** to religions and worldviews in an informed, rational and insightful way.

(REC 2013b, p 13)

The term 'religious literacy' is a metaphor, connecting to the skills of being able to read, write and communicate. However, the beginning of reading and literacy are exactly that – the beginning. It is the teacher's task in literacy teaching to seek to develop pupils' skills of comprehension, analysis and enjoyment of texts. In RE it is the teacher's role to create a learning environment where engagement with religious material is valued as pupils develop the ability to read and appreciate different kinds of religious texts and sources such as myths, figurative language, symbols, narratives, letters, poetry, actions, art and drama. In short, pupils will study the way religious and non-religious people make sense of their world and articulate their beliefs. In RE, pupils will engage with the stories which are central to religion and worldview, noting the concepts in them and linking them across faiths. For example, young pupils can begin to develop their understanding of the concept of sacrifice in and through the story of Dogger by Shirley Hughes. They will then later turn to the Christian account of how Jesus is sacrificed on the cross and possibly link this to the Buddhist story of the Monkey King who makes his own body into a bridge so that others might escape but loses his life in the event.

Pause for thought

This chapter started with a display (Figure 1.1, p 2) of the Judeo-Christian account of creation found in the first few chapters of Genesis. Do you know this account or about how other religions believe the world came to be? What is your own explanation and what might be those of the children you teach? Pupils could make a soundscape of the accounts of creation from different religions, choosing different instruments and celebrating the variety of the world. Some Christians take part in rogation where they walk round the boundary of a place to ask God's blessing. Children could walk round their 'boundary', saying what they are grateful for and how they intend to care for the place in order to be good stewards.

Religious literacy refers to that ability to understand the complexities of religious systems and people's ways of life. A religiously literate person understands that religions, although based on teachings that may not change, are internally diverse and movable in expression. As they become more religiously literate, pupils can begin to understand how religions will always embrace the mysterious and unpredictable, and so RE that supports its development will not be safe and risk-free but edgy. To become religiously literate means pupils can begin to question the legitimacy of claims in different faiths and be unafraid to discuss and deepen discussion about belief. Erricker maintains that religiously literate pupils will become 'discerning and critical about the value of religion, develop their own emergent worldviews and values and be constructively critical citizens within the social environment they will shape in the future' (Erricker et al. 2011, p 21).

So, it is not just knowing more about religions but having an improved conversation about them and the claims they make. Even the youngest pupils can talk in sophisticated ways about faith matters, as John Hull shows in his book *God-Talk with Young Children* (Hull 1991). Quinn, aged four, has this to say about the subject (Figure 1.3).

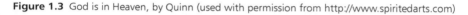

Figure 1.3 God is in Heaven, by Quinn (used with permission from http://www.spiritedarts.com)

God is in Heaven. He has very good listening ears because He can hear everyone when they pray. He has very good eyes as well because He is looking down at us.

Quinn

In summary, a religiously literate pupil will begin to talk about and discuss religions and worldviews in informed ways with increasing confidence, using religious vocabulary and terminology accurately. They will be able to draw similarities and differences between religions and worldviews developing a critical and a questioning approach, as they begin to form their own opinion having assessed different sides to an argument. Such pupils will maintain curiosity about religions and worldviews while beginning to question prejudice and bigotry and so a greater integration and a stronger sense of community can be formed. These are high aspirations, but in a classroom where these skills are developed, negative stereotypes will be challenged and education of a particular worth will happen.

Task two: The role of the teacher in developing pupils' religious literacy

The writers of the RE Framework maintain that 'pupils should gain and deploy the skills needed to understand, interpret and evaluate texts, sources of wisdom and authority and other evidence', and 'they learn to articulate clearly and coherently their personal beliefs, ideas, values and experiences while respecting the right of others to differ' (REC 2013a, p 14).

- What can the RE teacher plan, teach, model so that such objectives are realized?
- Consider the teacher's role in planning lessons that
  1 develop the pupils' skills of interpreting and evaluating texts and sources of wisdom;
  2 encourage pupils to articulate their own personal ideas, values and experiences clearly and coherently;
  3 help pupils develop respect for views that differ from their own.
- Think of practical ways that the classroom and learning might be organized through: the way classrooms are set up; displays developed; resources used; vocabulary extended; visitors invited; stereotypes challenged.

Clemmie, a PGCE student developed her first RE display with the pupils from a Catholic school in London about Pentecost and included the pupils' cinquain poetry on flames and doves, a Christian symbol for the Holy Spirit (Figure 1.4).

Teaching that will support pupils in developing religious literacy will help them to 'join the dots' to understand what it is to be a Muslim, Christian, Humanist, Jew, Hindu, Buddhist or Sikh. So, teachers will avoid teaching isolated fragments that leave the pupil confused and lacking the necessary frameworks for making sense of

Figure 1.4 Pentecost

the world, religion and worldviews. Informed teachers realize how some common approaches to learning about religion can lead to simplistic and inaccurate representations of religion and be mindful that there are many highly educated bigots and racists. Therefore, they seek to perpetuate an education of a kind where such attitudes are less likely to be thoughtlessly reproduced by those they teach. Developing such teaching should give pupils the space to reflect on why material covered in RE matters to them personally, and why it matters to other people, to the world now and in the future to their society, and to their future.

How can RE contribute to a child's whole development?

Through learning in RE, pupils can develop many skills and attitudes that are vital for learning throughout the curriculum and so benefit their whole development as people. An acronym that some have found helpful when planning good RE is CASK: relating to the development of Concepts, Attitudes, Skills and Knowledge. These aspects of learning in RE are revisited throughout the book and are just introduced here.

Concepts

A concept is a 'big idea', or an idea that is at the centre of a whole set of ideas, or at the centre of a 'theory' – a network of connected ideas. Some think of a concept as 'an idea with friends' or 'an idea of a class of objects'. In RE, ideas are introduced that teachers and pupils will return to again and again, developing a deeper or wider understanding of them every time. Concepts are revisited and taught about in increasing complexity and this is the basis of the spiral curriculum. Many who write about RE favour what is called conceptual enquiry, where the big ideas in religions and worldviews become the focus of learning and this approach is helpful in avoiding a fragmented approach to teaching in RE. In developing pupils' knowledge and understanding, wise teachers may adopt a pedagogy of conceptual enquiry rather than one based on the acquisition of propositional RE knowledge. Cooling (1994) and Erricker et al. (2011), the creators of *Understanding Christianity* (http://www.understandingchristianity.org.uk) and others have developed such approaches to RE and these will be discussed more throughout this book. These authors identify general concepts that are derived from shared human experience, concepts that are common across several religions or worldviews and include those that are identified in specific religions or worldviews.

Some examples of concepts used in RE are the following:

- Concepts that are part of shared human experience, such as celebration, remembrance or peace.
- Concepts that are shared across religions and worldviews, such as pilgrimage, worship or rites of passage.
- Concepts that are the domain of a particular religion, such as Trinity, Dharma or Torah.

You might want to think about other RE concepts, and into which of these categories they might fit. And you could take some of the concepts that have a special place in a particular religion, and consider how you might begin to link with what the pupils already know and experience in their own lives (those concepts that emerge from shared human experience) and consider how you might begin a lesson to introduce and explore those concepts. Examples might include the following:

- Sacrament (an outward sign of inner belief or blessing expressed in different ways by the Christian church);
- Ibadah (Worship in Islam);
- Mitzvah (the Jewish commands – there are 613 in the first five books called the Pentateuch: Genesis, Exodus, Leviticus, Numbers, Deuteronomy).

After this, you could go on to the 'A' of CASK: *attitudes*.

Attitudes

An attitude is a disposition to think or act in a particular way in relation to oneself and other individuals or groups or to events. Some attitudes that might be developed in

RE are open-mindedness, respect, reverence, courage, commitment, awe and wonder, discernment, empathy and tolerance.

- About the final two, what do you think is the difference between empathy and tolerance?
- Consider whether one is better than the other.
- What other attitudes or feelings are associated with these two words, and why? The question becomes how transferable these attitudes can be.
- How can tolerance or empathy be developed in the classroom in two ways?

Suppose the pupils are learning in RE through a module entitled *Welcoming Babies*. They have just watched a short clip about aqiqah. This shows a baby in a Muslim household who is only a few weeks old. The Father says the words of the Shahada into the baby's ear and then wets and shaves the baby's head. He collects the hair and weighs it on the scales to see how heavy it is. He explains that the same weight in gold will be substituted for the hair and the money given to an orphanage in the name of the child. The child is therefore, from the earliest time, exposed to two of the five pillars of Islam: Shahada, the declaration of faith, and Zakat, giving to charity.

While the video is playing, the teacher notes that some of the pupils are giggling and saying inappropriate things to each other about the Muslim family. What do you think the teacher should do in response? What questions should s/he ask the pupils at the end of the video? What could s/he do to help the pupils develop respect for the family and their way of expressing their faith and beliefs?

Following on from attitudes, consider the 'S' of CASK: *skills*.

Skills

A skill is an ability developed through training and practice and in RE the following skills (and plenty more) can be nurtured: communication, investigation, interpretation, information processing, reasoning, enquiry, creative thinking, critical thinking and evaluation.

You have already discerned some of the skills that the RE Council advocate developing in RE – skills that will be revisited throughout this book. You might like to think of different ways that investigation skills could be developed through:

- showing pupils some artefacts taken from the scenario about aqiqah – a set of scales, a razor, some hair and gold jewellery and asking them how these might be used by a Muslim family to express what they believe;
- providing clues so that the pupils might investigate: Christian Baptism – Jewish Shabbat – Hindu puja.

Knowledge

There are different kinds of knowledge and although RE is more than mere acquisition of knowledge, nonetheless, developing knowledge with understanding is a very important aspect of good RE. Some trainee teachers maintain that there are no right or wrong answers in RE as if this makes the subject unique and more valuable, but this is not completely accurate: Jesus was not Muhammad's brother; Sikhs do not generally worship in a cathedral; Christians do not usually wear the 5Ks. Here are two forms of knowledge that can be developed in effective RE:

- Propositional knowledge – that is, knowing things about religion and worldviews; that the holy book in Sikhism is the Guru Granth Sahib and it is treated with the utmost respect in the Gurdwara and by its readers as a living guru. There are helpful apps such as *REdefinitions* (from https://itunes.apple.com/gb/app/re-definitions/id1333493297?mt=8 or https://play.google.com/store/apps/details?id=com.ctvc.redefinitions) which can supply you with key items of such knowledge.

- Personal and tacit knowledge – it has been said that we know much more than we can say; pupils can be encouraged to articulate what they believe about some of the ultimate questions and mysteries of life and death.

Task three: Forms of knowledge

Consider different forms of knowledge:

- What type of knowledge do you think most teachers are more comfortable in developing in RE and why?
- Which form of knowledge do you think is easiest to assess and why? Does this make this form of knowledge more valuable? Do we value what we assess or do we assess what we value?
- How can pupils be encouraged to learn about and learn from religions and worldviews?

You might like to consider other forms of knowledge and their place in good RE, such as logical, procedural, semantic, systematic, empirical and somatic forms.

Having discerned some of the main aims of RE, the need to develop religious literacy, the place of CASK and some forms of knowledge, what follows are several activities that will help you consider your own reflective approach to mastering the subject. As all good teaching begins with the existing knowledge of the learner, the first few questions ask you to reflect on what you think about RE now, based on any previous engagement you may have with the subject.

Many trainee teachers who answer similar questions to these do not recall many positive memories of primary RE conducted in the classroom. They do, however, remember trips to places of worship and visitors from the religious traditions who were invited into school. Most memories of this type of RE are very good, but others are poor, especially when the visitor or community speaker has usurped their position in school to assume a 'soap-box' stand. Others remember instances where creative arts were used, or times when they were asked to think critically about the RE material and give opinions about what they thought and learned from each other. The most impoverished RE that is recalled involves the teacher reading a text and asking the pupils to rewrite the story and draw a picture. Such RE is rarely remembered fondly: words like 'boring' and 'unimaginative' are used. Listen to these comments (chosen for their negativity) from a few postgraduate ITT students and consider whether they resonate with your thoughts and experience:

I hated RE – it was so boring – we were never asked of our opinion and nobody seemed interested in knowing what we thought.

RE was mostly about listening to a Bible story and then being asked to rewrite it in our own words. The only creative thing about the lessons was that we got to draw a picture.

Even at a young age, I knew that I was not being asked to use my brain. …
I wanted to discuss the big questions in RE – instead we had stories about sharing our toys and sweets – just a mishmash of social training with a bit of morality thrown in.

CASE STUDY: A Pictorial Metaphor

Some trainees discover that it is useful to find a metaphor that helps them discern their initial feelings towards teaching RE. They are in good company. Comenius in the seventeenth century saw education like tending a garden, Freire (1993) in the twentieth century was against what he called the banking system of education, and Jesus used images and phenomena from everyday life to talk about what cannot be appreciated with the senses alone. Metaphor, when used wisely, helps us understand things in new and refreshed ways, giving greater clarity and the ability to reconsider existing assumptions.

Think about your own attitude towards teaching RE and choose an image in the form of a painting, cartoon or photograph that helps you articulate your feelings. Write a short narrative to accompany your choice and keep this safe, so that you can return to it in the future. In the last chapter of this book there will be some examples of how trainee teachers have developed in their thinking about teaching RE over time. The trainees who complete this activity before and after learning about what it is to be a teacher of RE discover that it helps them to reflect on their development and any transition in their attitudes/feelings because of their learning. These images have been called Pictorial Transitionary Metaphors by Maria James and emergent teachers have found this use of pictures a valuable reflective strategy.

Here are some initial, first metaphors used by people as they started to think about themselves as RE teachers and the reasons that they gave for their choices. Do any of these ideas resonate with you? Sadly, for copyright reasons we cannot include the images themselves but you can find them on https://images.google.com/.

- Nick chose an image of a Native American walking through a wooded glade and looking up into the sky through the trees with an attitude of awe and wonder. He wrote:

  I didn't enjoy RE. I did not like learning about religion and the thought of teaching it did not appeal in the slightest. I have some experience of RE in the classroom as I was a TA in a class and had to help out a supply teacher with RE in an unruly class last lesson every Friday afternoon. I held a negative view, possibly because of his methods, which mostly included getting pupils to colour a different worksheet on each religion and maybe watch a video or 2 every now and again. Very boring and the pupils didn't like it much either!

      I chose this painting because I feel that RE is too big a subject to tackle without sufficient knowledge or understanding of it and the world religions. I feel it is too much to focus on parts of it and it would always be wishy washy. Although I know it is about awe and wonder – I feel overwhelmed about how much I need to know.

- Amy chose Edvard Munch's *The Scream* (1893).

  This shows how I initially felt about teaching RE when I was even wary about whether the subject has a place in the National Curriculum. The anxiety depicted in this portrait emulates the strong feelings I held about the subject and thoughts such as 'Should we be imposing our views on young, impressionable minds?', 'How can I teach about a religion I do not know if I believe in?', 'How can I teach about faith and tradition without being hypocritical?'.

- Camilla chose Sylvia Edwards's *Labyrinth Medallian*.

  My image is *Labyrinth Medallian* by Sylvia Edwards. I considered RE to be a rich, colourful and diverse subject with many different influences. I was positive about learning more about RE and was embracing its richness and multi-culturism. Interestingly as I was reading up about Sylvia Edwards it said that she draws on her wide travels as an illustrator and journalist as a source of inspiration for her paintings. Her work is richly decorative a quality she ascribes to her years spent in Iran in close appreciation of Islamic art. The Art critic Mel Gooding has written of her work: Broadly speaking there have been two aspects to Sylvia Edwards art: on the one hand there has been a persistent impulse to the sensuous celebration of the visible world; on the other a mystical even visionary tendency to a refined dream-like representation of symbolic figures engaged in an enigmatic spiritual drama. I liked the way Mel Gooding spoke about her work as having a mystical tendency with symbolic figures engaged in a spiritual drama. I looked back at the painting and could see the symbolism and how it related to RE. I like the idea that subconsciously I may have picked up on this spirituality when choosing an image that I thought represented RE.

Through their choice of images, some primary trainees reveal that they have misgivings or anxieties about teaching RE in school. Through talking with them, several reasons emerge for these concerns. One reason is that teachers see religion as the cause of much strife and warfare in society and therefore not an appropriate subject for young pupils. Others find it difficult to appreciate the relevance that ancient teachings and practices hold for the twenty-first-century child. Think about your own experiences of RE and how these affect your current view of the subject:

- What are your memories of primary RE from your own schooling?
- What recent RE have you witnessed in school?
- What are the main differences between your own primary RE and the RE you have recently witnessed?
- What five words would you use to describe the purpose and quality of what you have seen?
- How confident do you feel to teach aspects of Christianity and why?
- How secure do you feel in teaching about Buddhism, Hinduism, Islam, Judaism, Sikhism, Humanism or other worldviews, and why?
- What can and will you do about this? (The recommended reading at the end of this chapter may help you.)
- What influence do you think your previous experience of being taught RE has on your present approach/attitude to teaching the subject?

Task four: Issues in teaching primary RE as a non-specialist

To consider some of these misgivings, imagine that you are the RE subject coordinator in a primary school who oversees and guides colleagues. A Newly Qualified Teacher joins the staff and is asked to teach RE for an hour a week but before their RE lesson, this colleague appears at your door and expresses concerns about teaching the subject. What do you imagine that s/he says and how would you respond to allay these fears and to reassure, encourage and empower your new, inexperienced colleague? In the box below are some of the most common issues that are raised but you might think of some others. Try to complete the missing sections. Remember that not all questions have neat or satisfactory answers and people may have to learn to live with conflict and dissonance. This is part of the learning curve in becoming a courageous RE teacher. RE should not and cannot be sanitized. The missing sections on the left are the potential questions or issues that the new teacher might have and the right-hand section contains the response and advice that the subject coordinator might give.

Issue raised	Response and advice
'I have no faith myself and so would find it hard to teach about what I do not believe or think is valuable.'	Response:
Issue	'Although you may have a very strong personal faith, you are to be a professional teacher. The aims of RE do not encapsulate trying to make pupils Christian, Sikh or Humanist but rather RE seeks to teach pupils about religion so that they may consider their own lives and beliefs in the light of these. Pupils need to learn to make their own considered and informed decisions in life.'
'I am afraid of causing offence through misrepresenting an aspect of faith through either ignorance or misunderstanding.'	Response:
'I am worried that the pupils – even the youngest – will know more than me about religion.'	Response:
Issue	'Begin with one religion and take a couple of topics and learn about those to start with. You will find that many religions have similar themes. There are some excellent books to help you learn about religions such as Geoff Teece's book (Teece 2001). If you were teaching Year 6 maths on Friday and did not feel you understood the work you would do your homework. Why should it be any different with RE?'
'I think religion is a personal affair and should not be taught in school. After all, RE in school doesn't happen in some major countries like America.'	Response:

These and other issues are real hindrances rather than red herrings for many who train to teach primary RE, and so deserve more consideration here. Many student teachers are overwhelmed by the amount of material they think they will need to learn. This is understandable, as religions and worldviews are vastly varied and complex. If this is your concern, then what Blaylock has to say will be of comfort. He maintains that RE teachers often need to *do less* but to *do it with integrity*. Blaylock supports careful curriculum selection 'so that we don't seek to show children everything about Sikhism in RE – but what we do show them should be authentic, potentially profound, and connected to their own questions and concerns' (Blaylock 2004, p 62).

Some teachers claim that because they do not have a faith, this helps them to teach RE from a purely objective standpoint or helps them understand many in the classroom who also do not claim affiliation to a particular religion or worldview. Others argue that having a religious faith is an advantage. Revell and Walters (2010) researched Christian and secular trainee teachers' approaches to their faith in the classroom. They found that those who self-identified as not religious felt that

> the sharing of agnosticism / religious doubt or atheism could have positive effects with the class. Without exception, these students located their positive attribute in the role of RE as providing a space for pupils to consider their own spiritual journeys.
>
> (Revell and Walters 2010, p 21)

The two authors recommend that

> all student RE teachers may benefit from being encouraged to problematise and critically reflect on key assumptions about the nature of objectivity and neutrality as a way of considering a wider range of pedagogies in the classroom.
>
> (Revell and Walters 2010, p 4)

They suggest that all believers (including atheist, agnostic, secular and Humanist groups) should acknowledge themselves as holding identifiable belief positions rather than neutral stances. Copley agrees with this, and additionally writes what a teacher's role in RE is and what it is not. 'The teacher's role ... is to promote awareness and understanding ... not to promote belief, whether religious or secular. In order to perform this role, the teacher is not required to be neutral, which would be humanly impossible, but rather to be skilled in their knowledge and understanding of the religious and secular values being presented' (Copley 2005, p 29).

It might be said that it is impossible to divorce ourselves from our values and beliefs as they are part of the weft and warp of our very being. The question is how we live with, present and use these in the classroom. Cooling (http://www.rethinking. co.uk) maintains that RE teachers cannot be neutral. Like everyone, they are shaped by their metanarratives which are the big stories that influence their understanding of life, themselves and their world. This means that the teacher of RE needs to be aware of their metanarrative because it will include what they believe about the nature and importance of religion in their own life and that of others. Cooling is convinced of the necessity for professional teachers to find a harmony between their personal metanarrative and their professional responsibilities, so that they can share the goals of the subject with others who have different narratives by which they live and work.

The RE classroom can create an environment where the dignity of difference can be celebrated and where pupils can learn and develop social skills through dealing with conflict. Without such potential disagreement, there would be little need to exercise and develop RE attitudes. The RE Council says that one of the purposes of RE is that pupils may 'learn to weigh up the value of wisdom from different sources, to develop and express their insights in response, and to agree or disagree respectfully' (REC 2013a, p 14). The question becomes whether those who hold religious convictions can be equitable in teaching about different religions and worldviews and whether those who do not have any religious conviction can do likewise.

Task five: The religious and non-religious RE teacher

What do you think about what these researchers discovered? Do you think the non-religious are better at teaching RE without bias? Do you think the religiously committed make the best RE teachers? Do you think it doesn't matter and depends on other factors?

- List the advantages and disadvantages of being religious, as an RE teacher, and the advantages and disadvantages of not being religious, as an RE teacher.
- Think about whether your own thinking has been challenged through your consideration.

Some trainee teachers are afraid of causing offence and many RE teachers will at some point (because of misunderstandings or lack of relevant knowledge) have inadvertently caused offence to pupils or their families. The humility and attitude of the teacher in responding to such offence, once highlighted, is important. RE teachers, like all teachers, should be able to say sorry and learn from their mistakes. It is humbling to be challenged in RE by a pupil in reception class, but teachers need to remember that their book-based knowledge is unlikely to be as rich or meaningful as the lived experience of the youngest child at home and in their religious community. Pupils and their families can – if willing – provide a teacher with a better understanding of their traditions than even the best textbooks. Pupils can be the teacher's richest resource, but they always must be asked and prepared first for any questions you would like to ask them in the classroom.

Faith and belief are considered a personal affair by many but are also often celebrated and exercised publicly. Take young pupils for a local walk and there will be testimony to faith through the locale's people, architecture, food stalls and monuments, to name a few ways. Religion is a visible phenomenon and it can be celebrated that this country is brave enough to include a subject in its curriculum that is risky, contentious and deals with issues that are about birth and death and everything in between.

CASE STUDY: Walking through the locale

On any walk through a village, town or city locale, teachers can list as many references there are to religion and belief. These might be places of worship, street names or names of a pub and the image they possess, war memorials or other statues. This can be a stimulus to thinking about how to prepare, organize and follow up such a learning walk with pupils and the sorts of questions that might be used to prepare them for the experience and encounter.

Summary

In this introductory chapter, the subject of RE and what it might achieve in the development of pupils has been introduced. Some of the main aims, skills and attitudes have been considered, including what it is to become religiously literate. Some of the main issues in teaching the subject have also been encountered. The acronym CASK has been used as one way to support your planning in RE. You have also begun a reflective consideration of your own relationship with the subject as you begin to think about yourself as a teacher responsible for effective RE. You will find it useful to read the texts recommended below as you continue to think about the subject and to gain further knowledge and understanding of the religions and worldviews that become the focus of effective primary RE.

Recommended reading

Blaylock, L (ed) (2004) *Representing Religions*; Birmingham: Christian Education.
Pett, S (ed) (2015) *Religious Education: The Teacher's Guide*; Birmingham: RE Today Services.
Teece, G (2001) *The Primary Teacher's Guide to Religious Education and Collective Worship*; Leamington Spa: Scholastic.

Chapter 2
Current Developments in Religious Education

Chapter objectives

- A brief history of RE in England and Wales
- Developments in teaching and learning in RE
- Systematic or thematic teaching?
- Learning about religions and learning from religion
- Legal requirements of the subject
- Learning objectives
- The current state of primary RE
- How can teachers positively contribute to pupils' enjoyment of RE?

Introduction

This chapter is shorter than the others. Its main aim is to provide you with a picture of where RE has come from, as its history may point towards its future. The writing refers to some of the current research on the subject and considers, briefly, how different schools get their syllabuses. Some approaches to teaching the subject are considered and note given to ways that teachers can positively contribute to pupils' enjoyment of RE.

In the last chapter, some of the main aims of effective RE were considered and you began to consider how you currently perceive yourself as a teacher of RE. This chapter begins by charting some of the history of the subject which should put the current state of RE in context. To know where RE is going, it is useful to see where it has come from. It is worth noting that, historically, Christian churches have been at the forefront of schooling in this country. By 1744 the Society for the Propagation of Christian Knowledge had established 2,054 schools; from 1791 Roman Catholic churches began setting up schools; in the late eighteenth century the Sunday School system was established; and the early nineteenth century saw Church of England, Roman Catholic and Free Church organizations setting up Teacher Training Colleges. All of this was long before the state became involved in schooling – notably from

1870 onwards. Against this background of involvement by churches, and Christianity being the dominant religion, it is unsurprising that Christianity was the primary focus of RE for many years in the UK. Until half a century ago, daily worship and Bible reading featured prominently in the everyday life of schools, and the Bible was the primary material for many pupils learning to read. Some of these traditions continue today especially in schools with a religious foundation (Figure 2.1).

A brief history of RE in England and Wales

In order to understand the current and future developments in RE, it is important to understand what has already happened. RE in every country is tied to the history

Figure 2.1 Clay cross, made by pupils of St Mary and St Thomas Aquinas Catholic Primary School, Gateshead

of the country – whether that is the anticlerical French Revolution of 1789 or the separation of church and state in the US constitution (which still means that RE is rarely taught in state schools in France or the United States), or the re-emergence of the power of the Orthodox Church in Russia in recent years (which means that RE is now on the national curriculum of Russia). In the UK, the Christian church and state are closely connected, and this has meant RE has been firmly established in the curriculum – but the nature of RE, and its relationship to Christianity, is still being argued about.

- The 1870 Forster Education Act set up 'county schools'. This Act included what is called the Cowper-Temple clause which stated 'No religious cate-chism or religious formulary which is distinctive of any particular denom-ination shall be taught in schools'. This meant while you could teach about Christian denominations such as Anglicanism and Methodism, you could not teach explicitly through a specific denomination – so no Hail Marys in a community school.

- During the mid-twentieth century, education authorities sought agreement among various religious and professional groups about what material should be covered in Religious Instruction (now called RE) and the development of the 'Agreed Syllabus' began – and was established in law in the 1944 Educa-tion Act.

- The 1944 Education Act made it mandatory for schools to adopt an RE sylla-bus and established RE as the only subject by law that had to be taught. This law also stipulated that each school day should begin with an act of collective worship, and established the legal requirement that schools support their pupils' spiritual development.

- The 1960s witnessed the development of more personal and social education and child-centred learning became increasingly important. The appropriate-ness of Bible-centred teaching came under scrutiny.

- Birmingham published the first multi-faith Agreed Syllabus in 1975.

- The Education Reform Act of 1988 (DES 1988) maintained that every Agreed Syllabus should 'reflect the fact that religious traditions in Great Britain are in the main Christian, whilst taking into account the teachings and practices of the other principal religions represented in Great Britain'. This requirement has been confirmed by the Education Acts of 1996, 1998 and 2010. The revised National Curriculum of 2013 stated, 'All state schools … must teach religious education … All schools must publish their curriculum by subject and academic year online' (DfE 2013, p 4).

- The law has remained the same, but various non-statutory guidance on RE has been provided:
  - In the 1990s, the principal religious groups advised the School Curriculum and Assessment Authority about appropriate teaching material and themes

emerging from their religions for the different stages of schooling. This consultation led to the development of two 'model' syllabuses for RE in 1994. One of these began with pupils' questions and one with religious material and so signified two different approaches to teaching RE.

○ In 2004 and 2010, further non-statutory guidance on RE was published by the Department for Education (DfE).

○ In 2013 the RE Council published 'A Curriculum Framework for RE' (REC 2013b). Many writers of new syllabuses follow the guidance of the document which reaffirms that 50 per cent of RE time should be used to study Christianity. This is non-statutory guidance. This report is the only full national review of the subject since 2004 by the Qualifications and Curriculum Authority (QCA 2004). The local Agreed Syllabus continues to be the only statutory requirement for teaching RE in community schools. Church schools follow Diocesan Agreed Syllabus guidelines and associated support materials and schemes. Academies and free schools have more flexibility over the curriculum (and their choice of an Agreed Syllabus), but must teach RE. Private schools are not covered by any legislation on the curriculum.

● Since 2016, the following developments have taken place:

○ RE Today Publications has published *Understanding Christianity* (http://www.understandingchristianity.org.uk), a major work building on previous work based on conceptual enquiry.

○ Wintersgill and others wrote 'Big Ideas in RE' (Wintersgill 2017). This described what principles and themes could be used to decide what to teach in RE.

○ A *Commission on RE* was set up in 2016, with a final report produced in 2018 (Commission on RE 2018, http://www.commissiononre.org.uk/).

The Big Ideas document (Wintersgill 2017) has a useful description of the 'purposes' of RE. These purposes are not all agreed in the various Agreed Syllabuses or the other documents that describe RE in schools, but they are a useful recent description of RE from a team made up of teachers, teacher educators, researchers and two people (Barbara Wintersgill herself and Alan Brine) who led on RE for Ofsted. This is what the document says:

The main purposes of RE should be to enable students to:

● understand the ideas, practices and contemporary manifestations of a diversity of religions and non-religious worldviews;

● understand how religions and beliefs are inextricably woven into, and influenced by, all dimensions of human experience;

● engage with questions raised about religions and beliefs, including questions about meaning and purpose in life, beliefs about God, ultimate reality, issues of right and wrong and what it means to be human;

- understand some of the main approaches to the study of religions;
- develop their own beliefs, ideas, practices, values and identities;
- develop the motivation, understanding and skills to make enquiring into religious questions a lifetime activity;
- flourish as responsible citizens of changing local, national and world communities with diverse religions and beliefs.

(Wintersgill 2017, p 6)

One of the major developments in the history of RE has been the establishment of the Local Agreed Syllabus, so it is worth taking time here to discuss this in more depth. Every local authority must set up a Standing Advisory Council on Religious Education (SACRE) to guide the RE and Collective Worship in its borough. The SACRE is made up of four main groups: Christian denominations other than the Church of England, and representatives of other (non-Christian) religions represented in the local area; the Church of England; teachers' associations and local authority representatives. Other members may be co-opted to the group but cannot exercise the same voting rights as the four main groups. In Kingston upon Thames, for example, a Ba'hai representative, Humanist and a member of a Christian group that supports the borough's schools with RE and Collective Worship attend as co-opted members. The SACRE typically meets three times a year.

An Agreed Syllabus for RE in a local authority sets out what schools (with the exceptions described above) should teach in RE. The text of the syllabus is composed by an Agreed Syllabus Conference which can include representatives of the various educational, religious and political groupings found in the area. This syllabus should be reviewed within five years of its publication to keep abreast of and incorporate recent developments in the subject. Many current Agreed Syllabuses follow the advice of the non-statutory National Framework (REC 2013b) and other non-statutory guidance. They typically include non-religious philosophies and worldviews as part of the scope of RE, although the current (2007 onwards) Agreed Syllabus for Birmingham is an exception, as it excludes 'secular Humanism and atheism' from its syllabus. Local Agreed Syllabuses incorporate clear strategies for progression in learning across the key stages and identify steps for progress.

Task one: Syllabuses

First, follow the links listed below and add to these syllabuses the Agreed Syllabus relevant to your school placements:

- The Local Agreed Syllabus from Kingston upon Thames: https://www.kingston.gov.uk/downloads/download/335/kingston_agreed_syllabus_for_religious_education

- The Local Agreed Syllabus for Birmingham: https://www.faithmakesa difference.co.uk/
- The Local Agreed Syllabus for Surrey: https://www.babcock-education. co.uk/4S/religious-education-in-surrey-schools

Compare and contrast the syllabuses and the guidance they provide for their schools.

Then, make a note of the main reasons why you think RE has gone through so many stages of development and change (much more than many other subjects). What main factors have dictated these changes? How far do you think these might be fuelled by the following: developments in educational thinking; an increased emphasis on child-centred learning; an evolving understanding of the purposes of RE; the changing religious, ethnic and social make-up of communities both locally and nationally.

Finally, there is increasing debate whether RE provision should be controlled nationally or locally. (RE has been legally required longer than any other subject, but always locally determined and never a subject of the National Curriculum.) Compile a list of the pros and cons of local provision as opposed to national provision for RE. Which arrangement do you think would be best and why? You will find summaries of some debates on this issue in the review by the REC (2013a, pp 35–6) and the report by Clarke and Woodhead (2015, pp 36–9, with briefer mention in Clarke and Woodhead 2018). More details of these readings can be found later in this chapter.

Having detailed the way in which many schools receive their syllabus for RE, we turn to the latest initiative in RE. In September 2018 the final report of the Commission on RE was published (Commission on RE 2018, https://www.commissiononre.org.uk/ final-report-religion-and-worldviews-the-way-forward-a-national-plan-for-re/), and this recommended the introduction of some important changes. Some of the major recommendations are that the subject's name should be changed to Religion and Worldviews, there should be a national entitlement (a bit like a national syllabus) for the subject, and there should be far more training for teachers of the subject. It will be interesting to see if any of the recommendations are enacted. Read the report, and see which changes you would like to see.

Developments in teaching and learning in RE

Over many years, different approaches to teaching RE have developed. Back in 1987, Bastide outlined three. He called these the Confessional, Factual and Understanding Religions approaches (Bastide 1987). Clarke and Woodhead (2015, pp 33–5) write about the differences between what they identify as 'Instruction', 'Formation' and 'Religious Education'.

Teaching RE in a 'confessional', 'instruction' or 'formation' way is more characteristic of schools with a faith foundation as these approaches can encourage pupils into adoption of a particular faith commitment. Parents have the legal right to send their pupils to schools with a religious foundation, and some do this so that their pupils' faith might be nurtured. However, even if this does sometimes take place, most schools with a religious foundation ensure that their pupils learn about other religions and worldviews.

The factual approach expects teachers to adopt a more neutral view to the truth or falsity of religions. In this way of teaching, religion is understood as a social phenomenon worthy of being studied because many people use it to make sense of and guide their lives, and because it influences society. This approach is quite sociological and it rejects the view that the teacher should nurture or commend any particular religion or worldview.

The understanding religions approach encourages a more empathetic approach to the study of religions and worldviews. Pupils explore deeper questions of meaning within religions for themselves and for those who follow the religion. This approach is more in line with what the REC (2013a) recommend as good practice. It encourages pupils to consider what it is to look at the world through Hindu eyes or from a Muslim, Christian or Humanist standpoint. It asks them to step tentatively and respectfully into the shoes of others so that they might learn about the religion and consider what they can take from the teachings for their own lives and belief. So, for example, when pupils attend the Sikh gurdwara and see the generosity and service of the Sikh community through the provision of the langar (the free kitchen), they are left wondering about how they treat others as they would like to be treated themselves. As they learn about sewa, the selfless service of the community as part of Sikh worship (performing an act of kindness without the expectation of reward), they are encouraged to think about how altruistic their lives are and the opportunities they have to serve others.

Pause for thought

Consider the RE teaching you have witnessed in schools. What type of school setting have you witnessed? Would you say that the teaching adopted the confessional, factual or understanding religions approach? What language might a school use if it wanted to *avoid* adopting a confessional approach to its teaching? This is a good point at which to consider what you have read about RE, and what that means for your own teaching.

Systematic or thematic teaching?

In different syllabuses, RE material can be arranged systematically or thematically, or it can combine elements of both arrangements.

Teaching RE systematically

- deals with one religion at a time through an exploration of the concepts and practices distinctive of that religion;
- seeks to build a holistic picture of one religion at a time;
- can be used more frequently in upper key stages.

Teaching RE thematically

- deals with cross-religious material;
- studies religions through themes such as holy books, places of worship and initiation rites;
- usually stresses similarities between religions;
- can be used more frequently in lower key stages.

Task two: Systematic or thematic?

Consider what you think about these two forms of delivery:

- What might be some of the themes included in the Early Years and Key Stage 1?
- Is teaching systematically or thematically better for Key Stage 1 learning?
- Which themes are covered in some of the locally Agreed Syllabuses that you have seen?
- Do you consider one form is better suited to the development of Key Stage 2 pupils?
- Which way of teaching is easier to assess and why?
- Make a list of the strengths and weaknesses of systematic and thematic RE teaching. Which way do you prefer and why?

With reference to this last point, consider the Jewish and Christian accounts of Noah's Ark. (The Muslim account of Noah's Ark, in sura 11 and 71 and elsewhere in the Qur'an, is different.) Write down the main concepts/themes included in this well-known narrative. (You can read it in Genesis Chapter 6, Verse 17 onwards in the Christian Bible, or a child's version such as the *Lion Storyteller Bible* (Hartman and Nagy 2008).) What did you decide? This story could be and has been linked with themes such as water, boats, animals, colours and the 2× table. However, for teaching RE, the story concerns concepts such as punishment, destruction, renewal, salvation and restoration. These are big complex issues. Religious material should be considered with integrity. If you want to use the account of Noah's Ark, then you should make use of the important religious themes and give the pupils an insight into religions. Otherwise it is just another story.

Figure 2.2 Noah's Ark, designed by pupils at St Mary and St Thomas Aquinas Catholic Primary School, Gateshead

What are some questions that could be asked to help pupils understand what Jews and Christians understand about themselves and their God through hearing the account? What age would you choose to teach the narrative of Noah's Ark? How would a secondary pupil react to studying the story and why (Figure 2.2)?

Learning about religions and learning from religion

Grimmitt introduced the idea of RE combining learning *about* and learning *from* religion/religions. Learning *about* religions is a more *factual* approach. Learning *from* religion involves more personal engagement, and is more of an approach focusing on *understanding* religions. This distinction has been included in many Agreed Sylla-buses since then, often as two separate attainment targets. This is what Grimmitt said he meant by these two attainment targets:

> When I speak about pupils learning about religion I am referring to what the pupils learn about the beliefs, teachings and practices of the great religious traditions of the world. I am also referring to what pupils learn about the nature and demands of ultimate questions, about the nature of a 'faith' response to ultimate questions.
>
> When I speak about learning from religion I am referring to what pupils learn from their studies in religion about themselves – about discerning ultimate questions and 'signals of transcendence' in their own experience and considering how they might respond to them. The process of learning from religion involves, I suggest, engaging two, though different, types of evaluation. Impersonal Evaluation involves being able to distinguish and make critical evaluations of truth claims, beliefs and practices of different religious traditions and of religion itself. ... Personal evaluation begins as an attempt to confront and evaluate religious beliefs and values and becomes a process of self-evaluation.
>
> (Grimmitt 1987, p 225)

More recently, syllabuses have not used these two attainment targets so often, partly because the framework from the REC (2013b) has omitted them. There are some good reasons for this omission, as some teachers concentrated only on 'learning about religions', while others just concentrated on 'learning from religion'. However, although these two attainment targets have been omitted, it is likely that the spirit of them will continue as teachers try to make meaningful links between the lives of pupils and the religious (and non-religious) material. There needs to be a body of core knowledge, as is the requirement nationally for other subjects, and this core knowledge needs to relate in some ways to the pupils' own lives and experiences to be accessible and of use.

Legal requirements of the subject

As you continue to reflect on your status as a teacher of RE, it is important for you to know the current legal status of the subject and your standing in teaching the subject. Here is a summary of points to note, some of which have already been covered:

- RE must be offered to all pupils of statutory school age.
- RE should 'reflect the fact that the religious traditions in Great Britain are in the main Christian whilst taking account of the teachings and practices of the other principal religions represented in Great Britain' (Education Reform Act 1988, DES 1988, chapter 40, part 1, section 8).

- RE in community schools should not be distinctive of any one denomination within any faith tradition.

- A reasonable amount of time should be made available to the teaching and study of RE.

- There is a clear distinction between RE and Collective Worship.

- Parents/guardians have the right to withdraw their pupils from RE.

- Teachers including head teachers have the right to withdraw from teaching or participating in RE.

- A school prospectus should include a clear statement on RE and must mention the right of withdrawal.

- Schools must report pupil progress and achievement in RE.

- It is the responsibility of the head teacher to ensure that the legal requirements with regard to RE are being met.

Learning objectives

So far in this chapter we have looked at approaches to RE, systematic and thematic teaching and attainment targets. Now we turn to the importance of writing appropriate learning objectives for RE. It is often said that if you get the learning objectives right for a lesson, much else follows. That is not to assume that pupils will *only* learn what you hope they will learn, as pupils often learn more – or different – things from what is expected. But it is helpful for everyone to have a clear focus to the learning and to have some idea of what you might be assessing.

Task three: Objectifying learning

Look at the following learning objectives for RE and consider whether you think they are good or bad as learning objectives. This is not about whether an activity described is appropriate, but whether the description is good of what you hope will be learned. A good rule-of-thumb for testing a learning objective is 'could a pupil a couple of years younger than those in this group learn this?' If the answer is yes, then the learning objective could probably be made more challenging. There are many other ways of judging learning objectives, such as whether the objectives are appropriate for a school, or whether the objectives make any assumptions about the religious position of the pupils. But there are clues in the list below. If you think the listed learning objectives are good, explain why. If they are bad, explain why, and write better learning objectives on the same topics. Remember that a learning objective is not the same as an activity: what are you wanting your pupils to *learn* from the lesson? All of the material included might take place in RE lessons, but you may have to research some of the material for yourself in order to complete the task. The first three are modelled for you:

Learning objective	Good or bad?
To be able to sequence the life of the Buddha	Bad – This is an activity rather than a learning objective. To translate this into a learning objective you might write: To know about how the life of the Buddha shows his importance for a Buddhist.
To understand the meaning behind the 5Ks	Could be better. How about the following? To understand why the 5Ks are important to Sikhs.
To become more respect-ful to Muslims	Not good, although it might seem good at first. There is an assumption implicit in the learning objective – that pupils currently do not respect Muslims. This may not be true of any of the pupils, and it is certainly unlikely to be true of your Muslim pupils. The attitude of respect should be nurtured in good RE, but how could you write a learning outcome that would target this, without making so many assumptions about pupils? Perhaps: To understand how to respect people who have different beliefs.
To draw an accurate pic-ture of the Sikh Golden Temple in Amritsar	
To develop an appreci-ation that Jesus is very special to Christians	
To understand why some Jews regularly attend synagogue	
To understand more about how God made the world	
To identify the reasons why most Muslims fast in Ramadan	
To write a poem or prayer about Bar Mitzvah	
To learn the ten commandments	
To know that Muslims pray five times a day	

To tell a story based on the parables of Jesus
To be able to make a model mosque
To be able to explain the reasons why Buddhists believe in non-violence
To enjoy the story of Noah's Ark

The current state of primary RE

The writers of one important recent review of RE said the following:

> RE has much to celebrate and the APPG [the All-Party Parliamentary Group on Religious Education] report [APPGRE 2013] refers to the 'overall gradual improvement in the provision for and quality of RE'. Ofsted has reported that there is good and outstanding practice in both primary and secondary schools and in schools where RE is taught well, pupils in general receive it with enthusiasm and respect.
>
> (REC 2013a, p 29)

As the expert panel for this review suggests 'There has never been a "golden age"' for RE; however, 'In a number of schools – primary, secondary and special – RE is identified by HMI as a subject that makes an important contribution to whole school priorities' (REC 2013a, p 58). This is good news and shows how effective RE can impact the whole curriculum.

Clarke and Woodhead (2015, 2018) discuss their research into RE, and call for changes to be made to RE as they believe the present legislation concerning the subject to be outdated. They bemoan the fact that RE is treated differently to other subjects, sometimes for the better, sometimes the poorer, and argue for the subject to be on the same footing as other curriculum subjects. They support the legitimate inclusion and learning about secular Humanism and other non-religious life stances, arguing that these perspectives should be treated in the same way as religions. They show that 'roughly equal numbers of younger people in Britain today report having "no-religion" as report having a religion' (Clarke and Woodhead 2015, p 8) and this is their main rationale for their viewpoint. They recommend the following:

- Changing the title 'Religious Education' to 'Religious and Moral Education';
- Making the RE syllabus in county and voluntary schools nationally rather than locally managed;

- Creating a new National Standing Advisory Council for Religious Education (NASACRE) to oversee the creation of a national syllabus for RE (there is already an RE committee called NASACRE, but this new one would have a different role);
- Facilitating SACREs to exercise a role of support to oversee a national RE syllabus;
- Developing community cohesion as a focus of RE that should be inspected by Ofsted.

Task four: More changes?

- What do you think are the advantages and disadvantages of changing the name of RE, as Clarke and Woodhead suggest?
- What do you think are the advantages and disadvantages of making community cohesion the focus of RE and its inspection, as Clarke and Woodhead suggest?

Eva writes the following (Figure 2.3):

My artwork is spiritual because it shows many international religious people meeting up together. I think it shows that Britain could be a rainbow nation because it shows each person is unique to make a religious rainbow. My inspiration comes from many 'colourful' religions.

Eva appears to understand the importance of this cohesion in some way.

Figure 2.3 A rainbow nation? (used with permission from http://www.spiritedarts.com)

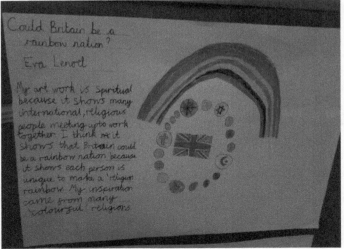

How can teachers positively contribute to pupils' enjoyment of RE?

The rest of this book takes this theme forward in showing good examples of effective RE by

- making the material relevant,
- involving pupils in their learning,
- introducing the real face of religion in the form of visits and visitors,
- planning dialogical RE by introducing discussion points through debate,
- using exciting resources such as art, theatre, videos, artefacts and dance,
- building a big picture of a religion,
- using the element of surprise,
- using different pedagogies – these will be covered throughout the book in the various chapters.

Pause for thought

The end of this chapter is a good time to pause and recall what you have come to know about RE so far. Because of the complicated statutory position of RE, there is a lot of uncertainty surrounding the subject. Decide whether the following statements are true or false. Do this before you look at the answers that follow.

1 Each local authority must write its own RE syllabus.	7 The subject is legally called Religious Instruction.
2 Teachers do not have to teach RE.	8 RE is a part of the basic curriculum.
3 There are no specific time allocations given to RE.	9 National statutory RE syllabuses have been produced by the government.
4 Parents have the right to withdraw their children from school to receive RE from elsewhere if they wish.	10 The teaching about specific denominations like Baptism, Methodism and Anglicanism is permissible.
5 Parents have the right to withdraw their children from parts of the RE syllabus they are not happy with.	11 RE can be delivered during Collective Worship time.
6 RE is about teaching Christianity and the other principal religions represented in Great Britain.	12 There is no legal requirement to report to parents about their child's progress in RE.

1 True – It is the Standing Advisory Council (SACRE) that provides their local Agreed Syllabus through their formation of a group called the Agreed Syllabus Conference.

2 True – Teachers can withdraw from teaching the subject. In some instances, teachers 'swap' subjects. However, RE must be taught as part of the curriculum.

3 False – The locally Agreed Syllabus normally addresses the time that should be spent on RE.

4 False – This is inaccurate. Parents cannot remove their children from school for RE – this would be very difficult to manage. The class teacher remains responsible for the children who may be withdrawn from parts of RE and should find ways for children to continue to learn during these times of withdrawal.

5 True – This one is accurate.

6 True – This is stated in the Education Reform Act of 1988 and maintained since then with the additional expectation that non-religious worldviews are covered by RE.

7 False – This is incorrect, the subject is currently called Religious Education.

8 True – The full curriculum is made up of the National Curriculum and RE.

9 False – There has been much non-statutory guidance and the RE Council have written a non-statutory National Framework for RE (REC 2013b). However, watch this space.

10 True – Teachers may teach about different denominations within the religions but not through them. Schools with a religious foundation may teach this way, so the teaching in a Catholic School will be based on Catholic teachings and principles.

11 False – Collective Worship is a different thing to RE. Certain themes might be introduced in Collective Worship time, but this is not the time for age-appropriate and progressive RE.

12 False – There is a legal requirement to report to parents about children's progress in RE. Currently, most syllabuses do not now include levels. There is a desire to bring a parity between RE and the rest of the curriculum subjects, so the RE world awaits guidance.

Summary

This chapter began with a history of RE. Different approaches and ways to teach the subject have been outlined including the use of the two attainment targets introduced by Grimmitt. Do you sense that you are beginning to understand more about how

RE is managed and taught as well as more of yourself as a teacher of the subject? We hope so. Do you now feel more confident to write appropriate aims for RE? How did you do in the final quiz?

Recommended reading

Clarke, C and Woodhead, L (2015) *A New Settlement: Religion and Belief in Schools*; London: Westminster Faith Debates (also available online at http://www.faithdebates.org.uk).

Clarke, C and Woodhead, L (2018) *A New Settlement Revised: Religion and Belief in Schools*; London: Westminster Faith Debates (also available online at http://www.faith debates.org.uk).

Commission on RE (2018) *Final Report: Religion and Worldviews: The Way Forward: A National Plan for RE*; London: Religious Education Council of England and Wales.

Wintersgill, B (ed) (2017) *Big Ideas for Religious Education*; Exeter: University of Exeter.

Chapter 3
Religious Education as an Irresistible Activity

Chapter objectives

- What does dynamic and irresistible RE look like?
- Creativity and curiosity in dynamic and irresistible RE
- What does Ofsted say about how Christianity is taught?
- How can curiosity be raised through teaching Christianity creatively?
- Seeing the big picture
- Being creative is a disciplined process

Introduction

In the last two chapters the irresistible subject that is RE has been introduced. You have continued learning about being a teacher of RE through encountering the history of RE, some of its main aims and some of the teaching approaches and forms of delivery. This chapter, which focuses mostly on the teaching of Christianity, begins to consider ways that RE may be taught creatively, drawing on pupils' curiosity. The notion of pupils building up a big picture in RE rather than dealing with fragmented and dislocated pieces of information is a central theme of this chapter.

What does dynamic and irresistible RE look like?

Having looked at the status and legal standing of RE and considered yourself more as a teacher of the subject, this chapter helps you to begin to explore what dynamic and irresistible RE looks like, with an emphasis on how Christianity might be taught in ways that promote pupils' curiosity and creativity. Christianity is chosen here, as certain inspections reveal (e.g. Ofsted 2010) and some research (e.g. Hayward 2007) shows that this religion is often taught without flair and secure teacher background knowledge. The chapter considers how innate curiosity and creativity in pupils might be nurtured even more through effective teaching in RE, and certain models for teaching and learning in Christianity that may help to develop these aspects are introduced.

The sculptor Henry Moore understood that in coming to know something for what it is, thinking about what it is *not* can be helpful: 'to know one thing, you must know the opposite'. This is true of religion: to know Christianity, you need to know other religious and non-religious systems. And it is just as true of creativity. It is not only the domain of the acclaimed artist or the skilled musician but a characteristic of being human. It could be said that creativity is energizing, empowering and risky, as well as exciting and dynamic, but equally it needs to be disciplined – as we argue later. As Desailly notes, it does not always have to be about the unique but concerns 'both generating new ideas and synthesising a variety of other peoples' ideas into a new understanding … [so c]reativity involves finding patterns, researching and hypothesising' (Desailly 2015, p 4). The creative person therefore develops transferable intellectual and academic skills. Can creativity be developed and nurtured and if it can, how? How can RE be taught in creative and exciting ways that capture the pupils' curiosity?

Ken Robinson tells a story of a child who sits drawing in class. When the teacher inquires what the child is drawing, the pupil replies 'I'm drawing a picture of God'. The teacher replies 'But nobody knows what God looks like', to which the child replies 'They will in a minute' (https://www.ted.com/talks/ken_robinson_says_schools_kill_creativity). The point being made here is that pupils are often creative, curious and unafraid to tackle big ideas and to offer their thinking to others, undaunted and unselfconsciously just as Quinn did in his image of God (Figure 1.3). But school can put them off. RE that takes account of this understanding is not safe: it takes the child and the teacher into unchartered territories, where the unpredictable may and probably should occur. In *The Lion, the Witch and the Wardrobe* (Lewis 2000), Susan asks Mrs Beaver about Aslan (who represents Jesus): is he safe? Mrs Beaver answers the following:

> 'Aslan is a lion – the Lion, the great Lion.'
>
> 'Ooh!' said Susan, 'I'd thought he was a man. Is he – quite safe? I shall feel rather nervous about meeting a lion.' …
>
> 'Safe?' said Mr Beaver. … 'Who said anything about safe? 'Course he isn't safe. But he's good. He's the King, I tell you.'

It takes courage to meet a lion, and it takes courage to be a teacher of effective RE. If you were asked to discuss the concept of God with a Year 4 pupil, how do you think you would fare? Look at these two images and narratives taken from the Spirited Arts website and wonder.

Monica (aged 8), Royal Grammar Junior School, Newcastle, *God is Looking Down*.

> God is looking down at us, and the two sides of the earth, Love and Hate. I have shown his face because no one knows what he looks like. I have drawn the entire

solar system because he controls the solar system and the universe. I have drawn the moon to say the smallest things can be big if you believe in God. (Figure 3.1)

Callum (aged 5), Wood End Park Academy, Hayes, *God in the Ocean*

I think God is in the ocean, because the ocean is so pretty and he thinks no one can find him there. He is invisible so the sharks cannot get him. (Figure 3.2)

Figure 3.1 God is looking down (used with permission from http://www.spiritedarts.com)

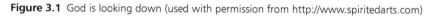

Figure 3.2 God in the ocean (used with permission from http://www.spiritedarts.com)

Despite initial misgivings and nervousness, you might be surprised by pupils' curiosity and willingness to engage with such a subject and experience how energizing such talk can be for them and for you. Such discussion allows pupils to speculate and wonder. Cavalletti notes that developing a pedagogy of wonder is crucial:

> Education to wonder is correlative with an education that helps us to go always more deeply into reality. If we skim over things we will never be surprised by them. Wonder is not an emotion of superficial people; it strikes root only in the person whose mind is able to settle and rest in things, in the person who is capable of stopping and looking.
>
> (Cavalletti 1992, p 139)

Those who work with pupils know that they are anything but superficial, but Cavalletti goes on to bemoan that much education today does not nurture the child's awe, wonder and sense of surprise. A child's sense of wonder will be quashed if it does not find a worthy object on which to dwell. The material of good RE supplies a stimulus for the development of this wonder, leading to deepened curiosity. Gaarder (1994) likens the curious child to the philosopher, maintaining that both have never quite got used to the world. Common to both the child and the philosopher is the faculty of wonder. Philosophy for Children (P4C, https://p4c.com) has become very popular and you may like to investigate this for yourself. The RE Council proposes pupils 'should be encouraged to be curious and to ask increasingly challenging questions about religion, belief, values and human life' (REC 2013a, p 21). It was Alice who declared things get 'curiouser and curiouser' in *Wonderland* (Carroll 1998)!

Pupils have an extraordinary capacity for creativity, and this faculty is as important to develop as their literacy, numeracy and other skills. In RE, as in other subjects, creative thinking cannot be rushed. Pupils require time to dwell on concepts and to have space and time to come to their own thinking about the ultimate questions and big issues of life. Effective RE can provide the space to facilitate such exploration, and this needs non-didactic forms of pedagogy that can lead to engaging and immersive learning. Ironically, to facilitate space in teaching RE, it is necessary to have structure and purpose. A door or window provides a space, but it must be framed to exist. RE can open doors and windows on what it means to be a person – a Christian, a Hindu, a Humanist.

> Thirty spokes share the wheel's hub;
> It is the center hole that makes it useful.
> Shape clay into a vessel;
> It is the space within that makes it useful.
> Cut doors and windows for a room;
> It is the holes which make it useful.
> Therefore benefit comes from what is there;
> Usefulness from what is not there.
>
> (Lao Tsu, Tao Te Ching, Chapter 13 verse 11, http://www. schrades.com/tao/taotext.cfm?TaoID=11)

So, what does dynamic and irresistible RE look like? It will have contrasts, opposites, contradictions. It will have brightness and it will have danger. It will have mystery and clarity. It will have an endless line of questions, and a thousand different answers to every question. RE should never be beige or bland or just 'nice'. Wars have been fought for and against religious beliefs: that is troubling, but it also says how important the presence or absence of religion is to people all around the world. If RE teaching is to reflect all of these contrasts, all of these different ways of life, all of these beliefs, it must be exciting, dynamic, irresistible and, most of all, creative. You should be curious about RE and all its mysteries (and you may also be a little scared and annoyed at times), and you will pass this on to your pupils.

Creativity and curiosity in dynamic and irresistible RE

The RE teacher who restricts RE lessons to reading a story from scripture, asking the pupils to retell the account in their own words and to drawing a picture of that story, is not allowing RE to be as creative or irresistible as it could be, nor are effective learning spaces being facilitated. The teacher who restricts RE lessons to asking the pupils to complete a cloze exercise following input about material from one of the principal religions represented in Great Britain is hardly allowing dynamic RE to emerge. Cutting, sticking and colouring all have their place, but when the main RE activity is to cut up a story board about a Bible narrative into sections, match the pieces to their corresponding captions and stick them back together again, it is not only the minute pieces of paper that get lost, the pupils' motivation and creativity can go missing too. Doing the same exercises on a computer is no better – even if at first it seems more exciting. Rather than completing such exercises and *regurgitating* RE material, Cooling and Cooling (2004) maintain that *reprocessing* covered information is the better way for pupils to learn. It is certainly more creative. These authors give numerous examples of activities that help pupils complete this act of reprocessing using Bible narratives. They suggest the following:

- Highlighting important words in a text and say why they are chosen.
- Turning a text into a drama.
- Creating a diagram for a story.
- Turning a text into a visual through designing a series of posters or banners.
- Creating music or lyrics from a religious text.
- Representing a religious concept as a symbol (or metaphor).
- Changing prose into poetry (http://www.stapleford-centre.org).

Such activities require the pupils to reveal their own interpretations of the learned material much better than the impoverished activities of cloze or reproductive activity. Sadly, Christianity can sometimes fall prey to lacklustre, regurgitative forms of teaching and learning in RE as the following true story indicates.

Pause for thought

As part of their RE Module, ITE students are to complete an activity about festivals. In completing an assessment, groups are required to present a festival from the principal religions represented in Great Britain, to indicate how they will teach about and from the festival in the classroom. The festivals are Diwali in Hinduism; Wesak in Buddhism; Passover in Judaism; Baisakhi in Sikhism; Eid-ul-fitr in Islam and Easter in Christianity.

The students randomly choose their festival from a bag and most seem content with their choice except the group that is allocated Christianity. These people appear rather disappointed and say so. Two weeks later, when the presentations are given, most are creative and innovative, but the Christian festival work appears lacklustre and less researched than the others and contains some inaccuracies. A few students are even flippant and somewhat disrespectful about the material presented.

- Why do you think the students were disappointed with their choice of Christian festival?
- Why was Easter less researched than the other festivals?
- Why was the flippancy in presenting this festival not evident in the other presentations?
- What should the tutor do to get the students as excited to teach Christianity as to teach other religions?

These questions about the quality of the presentation were posed to a different group of postgraduate ITE students. Here are some of their main responses. Do they resonate with the reasons you have given?

- Christianity is not seen as cool or fashionable, like Buddhism is. It's too commercial.
- Repetitive. Too familiar. It's not new and exciting. It's the everyday, and so the process of research is not exciting. What new things can we present that people will not already know? It's like we have been inoculated.
- There is an interest in non-Christian faiths in the UK because they are unfamiliar to many, and knowing about them allows you to understand your neighbour and local community – which is changing and can be unsettling or fascinating for some.

The main reason given by the group was that they felt the students believed they already knew all about Easter and so did not find it as exciting or challenging to research, resulting in less enthusiasm. However, it is often the case that assumed knowledge and understanding about Christianity is far less secure than the student teachers believe it to be.

CASE STUDY: Teaching Easter

Some trainee teachers find innovative ways of teaching about Easter and there are some excellent resources available.

- One teacher in Key Stage 1 taught about Palm Sunday using a box of Kinder eggs – each egg containing a symbol or object associated with the narrative such as a tiny palm leaf, a toy coat, donkey, a photograph of a happy child, a scowling adult and the word 'hosanna'. The teacher asked the pupils to 'crack' the egg and the account was pieced together. The last egg was left empty and the pupils asked what they would put in it following the story. They applied the idea to another aspect of the narrative and designed their own egg-box and contents.

- Another student showed a snippet from the Lion King when Scar, the wicked uncle, betrays Mufasa, Simba's Father, and the pupils discussed feelings to do with being let down by others and linked this with the account of Judas's betrayal of Jesus.

- Yet another teacher asked older pupils to order the events of Holy Week from 'newspaper headline' descriptions of the events printed on cards. On the back of the each of the headlines was a letter that spelled 'resurrection' when the pupils ordered the pieces correctly.

Some teachers use Bible Story Bags to help the pupils visualize the biblical narrative (http://www.stapleford-centre.org). Each unit in the book which covers a Christian story includes a reflection, optional prayer, follow-up activities, comprehensive background material and two scripts for younger and older pupils. See http://www.barnabasinschools.org for PowerPoint slides of how to use such a resource. Jane Whittington of the Guildford Diocese (https://www.cofeguildford.org.uk/) uses these resources and two examples are included below. She says the following:

I use a script that tells the story and place the object as I tell it Godly Play style. When I work with EYF children I then leave the items out for them to 'play with' / retell the stories themselves. I often use one about the Good Samaritan called the Road of Choices from this book which focusses on the choice that each character made and then leads into an excellent discussion about our choices and why we make them. Once the children have experienced a few of these reflective stories we have suggested them as something that the pupils could do as a learning activity. You have to be very clear what the point of a story or idea such as the beatitudes is, and it generates thoughtful work.

How would you use these scenes of Good Friday and Easter Sunday with young pupils? Try writing a script for one of the stories. *Godly Play*, mentioned in this extract, was developed by Jerome Berryman (Berryman 1991, and https://www. godlyplay.uk/). It was designed for Christian religious nurturing and follows the pattern of the Christian Eucharist in that pupils gather, engage, ask (wonder), respect, share and then leave. Some teachers have adapted it effectively for use in RE lessons, but care should be taken to present such work in a way that respects the various views of the pupils (Figures 3.3 and 3.4).

By the time pupils leave primary school, it is likely that they will have learned about, or at least encountered, Christmas and Easter seven times. It is therefore essential to teach about and from the festival in ever increasing complexity dependent on the age of the pupils. If this is not the case, the teacher risks the pupils muttering 'we've already done this' and therefore disengaging. This form of revisiting material is often referred to as the spiral curriculum (see Bruner 1977). Considering themes can be a successful way of 'spiralling up' the learning across the years. This is an occasion where good planning across the whole school will help

Figure 3.3 The crucifixion

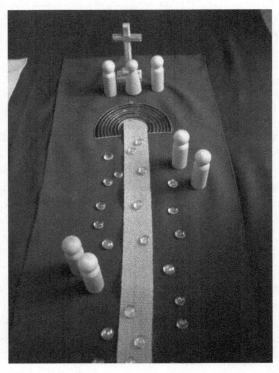

Figure 3.4 The empty tomb

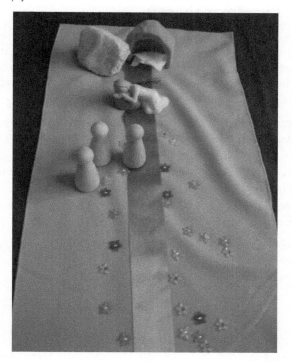

the whole RE curriculum. Cooling refers to a process he calls the onion method, maintaining the following:

> The aim is to make increasing intellectual and affective demands on pupils as they progress through their years of schooling. Rather like peeling away the layers of an onion until you reach its heart, this method facilitates an ever-deepening exploration of the same material.
>
> (http://www.stapleford-centre.org)

It could be argued that one never reaches the heart of the mystery of faith and belief, but this method ensures that taught material is age appropriate and progressive. As a starting point, as you begin to think about a festival, it may be helpful when planning, teaching and learning to consider it under the following four main headings (based on those suggested by RE Today Publications):

- The story/narrative behind the festival (sacred text or important event).
- The deeper beliefs behind the festival (theology and worldview).
- The customs and practices associated with the festival (ritual and tradition).
- The experiences of a twenty-first-century child (lived reality).

Task one: Christmas themes

To help you think about how you might teach about a Christian festival yourself, read the account of Christmas at the start of the New Testament Gospels of Matthew (starting with Mary being found to be pregnant) and Luke (starting with the angel Gabriel appearing to Mary). (There are some very good pupils' versions of the Bible.) Complete the following exercise:

- Write down as many themes for Christmas as you can, bearing in mind what has already been said about the choice of themes in this and the previous chapters.
- Decide which themes are more suited to Early Years and Foundation Stage, Key Stage 1 and Key Stage 2, and colour code them.
- Take one of the themes for each stage and consider how a series of three lessons might help you explore Christmas with the pupils.

You might like to start with a spider diagram and use it to chart your thinking about the themes.

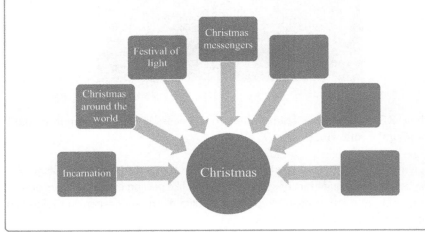

One clever teacher who wanted his pupils to understand the meaning of Christmas behind its associated paraphernalia placed a simple picture of the nativity on a board and obliterated it with the trappings of the festival; a turkey, tree, baubles and the like. As each item was removed the pupils talked about why the artefact was used at Christmas, sorting them into those that had religious significance and those without, until the simple picture was left and the pupils retold the biblical narrative.

One example of a Year 3 lesson on the topic of angels (as part of a Christmas theme) involved the teacher providing the pupils with a range of images to help them decide on words that they would use to describe an angel (of course angels appear in other religions apart from Christianity). The pupils chose adjectives such as shy, secretive, powerful and frightening. An atmosphere of reflection was skilfully created using music and silence. The pupils were then given some scenarios to extend their ideas, such as how they would greet an angel and what questions they would ask at the encounter. From this outline of the lesson, in what ways was this a good lesson, and how could it be improved?

Task two: Angels

Creative RE often incorporates links with other subjects such as music as in the example given above. Devise some other cross-curricular links for the theme of angels but be sure to maintain the RE focus and develop explicit knowledge and understanding of the biblical material. Plan for a series of three lessons. First, decide how you would introduce the biblical narrative to a Year 5 class to make this material central in the teaching. The questions and ideas are designed to help you plan.

1   What would your overall learning objective be for this series of lessons?

2   How would you progress the learning?

3   Which cross-curricular links would you develop? Here are some ideas – build on them:

- *Art* – What images would introduce the concept of angels? (e.g. Gormley's Angel of the North. Explore why the artist created this statue and discover angels in church architecture). For Key Stage 2 pupils there is a school's information pack available online (at https://www.gateshead. gov.uk/DocumentLibrary/Leisure/Angel/Angel%20Pack%20for%20 schools.doc). Pupils might design their own image suitable for a stained glass window, a kneeler in a church, a church banner. Encourage them to decide where they would choose to put their creation and why (*Art and Design*). Look at how one Gateshead school has used this structure in the creation of a display that represents the community (Figure 3.5).

- *Music* – What music could be included and why – how might more links with music, sound and silence be used? What music would angels like and why? What would angels sing and why? Investigate the angels' songs in the Bible and set them to music. Create a playlist of music for an angel, justifying the choice of each track.

- *Literacy* – What other adjectives might be used to describe an angel? Use these to write poetry of various kinds, for example haiku, acrostic.

- *Computing* – If an angel could tweet or put something on social media – what would their message be?

4   How and when do angels appear in the Christmas narrative? What is their role? Interrogate the following:

Luke 1:5–25 – John, Jesus's cousin, is foretold.

Luke 1:26–56 – Jesus's birth is foretold to Mary (the annunciation).

Matthew 1:18–25 – the angel speaks to Joseph about the baby Jesus.

Matthew 2:13–14 – an angel tells Joseph to flee from King Herod.

Luke 2:8–20 – the visit of the angels to the shepherds.

Consider the main messages of the angels.

Figure 3.5 The community

5   What do many Christians believe about angels? What is their role and
    why? Do some Christians believe that God still uses them? According to
    many Christians, when else does God send messages to people through
    angels? How else would a Christian say that God speaks to them? Do
    other religions have angels in them?

Jane Whittington, mentioned earlier in this chapter, organized an art exhibition of
angels at Guildford Cathedral. This resulted in a throng of two hundred angels from
forty-seven schools. (Search the web for reviews.) The angels were mostly made
of recyclable materials. It is valuable considering which of these angels may best
illustrate the various different descriptions of the activities of angels that are mentioned in the previous task or elsewhere in the Bible – with angels making their
first appearance in the first book, Genesis. Angels are also important in Judaism and
Islam, so curious pupils and teachers might explore how angels and their activities
are described in those traditions too.

Here are a few of the host: see Figures 3.6–3.9.

Figure 3.6 Angel 1, by Crookham CE Infant School, Fleet

Figure 3.7 Angel 2, by Potters Gate CE Primary School, Farnham

Figure 3.8 Angel 3, by Waverley Abbey CE Junior School, Farnham

Figure 3.9 Angel 4, by Christ Church CE Infant School

What does Ofsted say about how Christianity is taught?

In its various publications based on inspection of RE (Ofsted 2010, 2013), examples are given of effective and of impoverished RE. Ofsted notes that good practice 'integrated opportunities for reflection and creativity effectively within the process of enquiry which arose directly from pupils' engagement with religious material' (Ofsted 2013, p 23). This report maintains some improvements have been made to RE teaching over recent years, and there is plenty more to do, noting that 'RE teaching often fails to challenge and extend pupils' ability to explore fundamental questions about human life, religion and belief' (Ofsted 2013, p 4). Many of the schools visited 'did not pay sufficient attention to the progressive and systematic investigation of the core beliefs of Christianity' (Ofsted 2013, p 9). For example, in Christianity, some teachers are happy teaching about Christmas but omit Easter where, theologically, one does not make sense without the other. For example, the gift of myrrh might be used to rub on a baby's gums when teething, and also in funeral rites. And when Christianity is taught, material such as Jesus's parables are used to teach social or moral themes without mentioning their religious significance. Fragmented, unsystematic, teaching about Jesus means that pupils have little opportunity to understand the meaning and theological significance of his ministry. Understanding of the diversity within a religion may also remain unappreciated by the pupils – giving only one cultural perspective on what is a diverse and global religion. Pupils who belong to every religious and non-religious tradition – including Christian pupils – can be invited to share their understanding and practices in RE lessons.

Here is a description of a lesson. The focus was the healing of the blind man by Jesus:

- Teacher asks what a miracle is and whether the pupils can recall one.
- The story of the healing blind man is told.
- The purpose of the lesson is given – to imagine what it was to be blind.
- The pupils are shown a Braille alphabet and use a feely bag to imagine this.
- The main task is to write a poem about what they would miss if they were blind.
- The plenary involves more discussion, including how lucky sighted pupils are to have their sight.

What would you add to help the pupils engage with the religious significance of this biblical account? Can you think of how you might use pupils' questions in and for the learning? What are the challenges of using this miracle account? (The RE specialist and Christian minister John Hull, who was blind, has written of how negatively blindness is portrayed in the Bible, and how problematic this can be for blind people, in Hull 2013.)

Sometimes the opportunity to explore in RE through the use of effective questioning is not taken. This may be because teachers fear they will not be able to answer the questions and are afraid that ignorance will be exposed. Such teachers may believe they are there simply to 'deposit' knowledge into pupils – this is what Freire (1993) calls the 'banking' approach to education. This is a very impoverished view of how knowledge is 'acquired' and of the art of pedagogy. Teachers should be developing a pedagogy of questioning rather than just providing answers, and this approach has a good pedigree. As noted in Chapter 2, back in 1994 the School Curriculum and Assessment Authority (SCAA) produced two model syllabuses that SACREs could use in developing their own locally Agreed Syllabuses (SCAA 1994a, 1994b). One was called *Questions and Teachings*. This model began with the questions that religions pose and which can become the motivation for pupils to explore to formulate their own enquiries. Good teachers have always asked searching questions, including the leaders and founders of religions. Many times, Jesus responded to a question with another question causing the inquisitors to think through things for themselves. Questions can be provocative, causing normative assumptions to be questioned and challenged. And teachers 'knowing all the answers' is impossible in any subject – and clearly impossible in RE, where the world's greatest religious leaders and philosophers are still uncertain about, or disagree about, the possible answers to the biggest questions.

Although not used in school now since the demise of levels of attainment, some of the wording of the attainment levels for RE can be helpful in developing teaching and learning based on a pedagogy of question rather than answer and thus perpetuating curiosity. Progressive statements of attainment (taken from earlier level descriptors) might read as follows:

- Pupils talk about their own experiences and feelings, what they find interesting or puzzling. …
- [Pupils] recognise that some questions cause people to wonder and are difficult to answer.
- [Pupils] ask important questions about religion and beliefs, making links between their own and others' responses.
- Pupils raise, and suggest answers to, questions of identity, belonging, meaning, purpose, truth, values and commitments.
- Pupils ask, and suggest answers to, questions of identity, belonging, meaning, purpose and value, values and commitments, relating them to their own and others' lives. (QCA 2004, p 36)

We return to the need to ask challenging questions in Chapters 5 and 7.

Pause for thought

So, returning to the account of the blind man healed by Jesus and having considered the need for questioning in irresistible RE, did you decide to add to the lesson? First, ensure that you read the passage several times, taking the account recorded in the gospel of John Chapter 9. (You can also search for other Bible accounts of healings of the blind.) Here are some questions to guide your thinking:

- What will your main learning objective/s be for this lesson?
- What resources will you use?
- How will the pupils learn about the Bible account?
- How will pupils be enabled to ask questions about the narrative?
- What open-ended questions will you ask the pupils about the text?
- Consider questions asked in the story (there are at least a dozen). Who asks them and why? What questions would the pupils ask the blind man, Jesus, the parents, the Pharisees in an interview? The pupils might draw up a web or diagram showing these – noting question, questioner, reason, answer, new potential question. They might hot-seat a prepared visitor who acts as the healed man or another character.
- What difficult things does Jesus say? What did he say about himself and God? What do Christians believe about these claims? What do Christians believe the healing of the blind man teaches them about: God, Jesus, healing, the different reactions of the characters?
- Have the initial questions that the pupils had, been answered? Have others developed? Is it important for all our questions to be answered? Why or why not?
- What is faith?

Einstein wrote the following:

The important thing is not to stop questioning. Curiosity has its own reason for existence. One cannot help but be in awe when he [*sic*] contemplates the mysteries of eternity, of life, of the marvellous structure of reality. It is enough if one tries merely to comprehend a little of this mystery each day.

(Einstein 1955, p 64)

Pupils' curiosity is nurtured in good RE and this involves helping them to develop questions and consider possible answers for themselves. This means bringing them to the extremity of their existing knowledge so they need to find out. The teacher's role is in facilitating and supporting this exploration. Promoting curiosity can be scary for teachers, because many teachers think they need to know all the answers. Of course teachers know lots of things, and pupils always enjoy it when a teacher knows something really interesting. But a 'know-all' is not curious: someone who thinks they know everything will not want to learn more.

So, by being curious you are admitting that there is still lots you *don't* know. So *embrace your knowledge*, and, equally, *embrace your ignorance*. Never let your knowledge stand still, and always use your ignorance to fuel your curiosity. If you can develop those qualities in your pupils, RE really will be irresistible.

How can curiosity be raised through teaching Christianity creatively?

One aid to planning effective and creative RE that was developed in the 1990s (Cooling 1994) continues to be especially useful for teachers of RE. This model or framework is termed 'Concept Cracking' developed by Cooling and the Stapleford Project for RE. The Project was set up in 1986 by the Association of Christian Teachers in England (with materials at http://www.stapleford-centre.org). Cooling asks whether pupils can contend with big and difficult ideas and concepts in RE and believes that they can, providing that

- the ideas are presented in a way that makes sense to their world of experience;
- teaching methodologies take account of the ways pupils learn;
- fundamental ideas are taught as happens in other subjects such as in science;
- a 'concept rich' environment is created where the key ideas become a part of the pupils' world of experience;
- bridges are built between the pupils and the religious content;
- pupils do not retain simplistic understanding of big concepts, because subsequent enquiry and creative, age-appropriate, teaching enables them to gain a more sophisticated understanding.

On this last point, look at what Armstrong has to say, in the introduction to her book *A History of God*:

> My ideas about God were formed in childhood and did not keep abreast of my growing knowledge in other disciplines. I had revised simplistic childhood views of Father Christmas; I had come to a more mature understanding of the complexities of the human predicament than had been possible in kindergarten. Yet my early confused ideas about God had not been modified or developed.
>
> (Armstrong 1993, p 3)

Why do you think many adults stop learning and engaging in this way?

The major objective of the Stapleford Project was to marry theory with practice and produce materials which are accessible for the non-specialist teacher in community schools as well as schools with a religious foundation. This was because of the belief that some teachers are reluctant to present abstract religious ideas in RE, some teaching and learning is undemanding and non-progressive and an inappropriate use is made of Bible stories. When asked to teach the Biblical narrative, festival, belief or practice in Christianity, non-specialist teachers often do not have a framework to help them plan to teach the material in ways that retain the integrity and theological significance of the religious material. The help for understanding and planning that Cooling proposes is to unearth and crack the concepts of the religious story, practice, concept, belief or festival using the steps below:

Step 1: Unpack the beliefs – remember that this story/belief can also be preached in a church on a Sunday to a mature congregation and become the subject of exegesis and hermeneutics as well as being taught in a primary school by a non-specialist RE teacher.

Step 2: Select one or two beliefs/concepts to explore – these will be chosen by the wise teacher with reference to the age and aptitude of the pupils.

Step 3: Engage with pupils' experience – this will entail the teacher finding 'hooks' into the explicit religious material by earthing it into the pupils' experience and existing knowledge and so preparing them for the material they will encounter in the lesson.

Step 4: Religious and relevant – the religious material will be taught and the relevance of this in terms of what a believer would understand and what the pupils may learn in order to continue to develop their own beliefs and understanding.

These four steps spell out 'USER' (unpack, select, engage, religious and relevant). Here is an example of the way USER might be used.

CASE STUDY: Repentance

The Year 2 teacher was following the locally Agreed Syllabus directive to consider stories about people that Jesus met. This week the story was about Zacchaeus the tax collector. She read the account in both an adult Bible and the *Lion Storyteller Bible*. She thought about the beliefs behind the account and unpacked these (Step 1). The concepts of 'being sorry', change, repentance, salvation, conversion, sanctification, reconciliation and atonement were evident but because she had in mind the age and aptitude of her pupils she chose 'saying sorry' and change as the main concepts. She decided she would also introduce the pupils to the concept of repentance as a new RE word of the week (Step 2). She recognized that this is a universal story – equally fitting for a mature congregation in a church as well as her six and seven-year-old pupils. She wondered how to explore with the pupils what they already knew about saying sorry and being forgiven and decided to begin by using a familiar and daily scenario – the repentance and reconciliation necessary after most playtimes and saying sorry and meaning it and what this would look like (Step 3). Discussion would follow with the pupils about the feelings they had when they were forgiven and what happened when someone held a grudge. The pupils would be encouraged to think about any stories and television programmes that concerned the lesson's concepts. She decided she might also read the following poem. It is written by a primary pupil, wanting to put all her 'badness' into a box, and bury it.

The Bad Box

I will put in the box
Bad swearing and rudeness.
I will put in the box
Nasty kicking feet
And bad children, like me.

I will put in
My horrible shouting voice.
My box is made of dark green glass
And you lock it with a key
I will bury it under the ground.

Lesley Bull (aged eight) (from Stern 1995, p 58)

How do you think Lesley was feeling? Was she sorry? What would your class want to say to her? This teacher thought about how to introduce the religious and relevant material knowing she had prepared the pupils for what they would encounter (Step 4). She wanted to tell the story in a creative and imaginative way and so decided to use a story bag which held items that she would reveal throughout the telling. This included a bag of coins, a leaf, a plate, a sorry note and three more items. She wanted the pupils to grasp what Christians believe happened to change Zacchaeus and to understand how inner belief is expressed in outer action. She was wary of making this story into a moral homily so the pupils would only take away from the story that you mustn't steal – or that collecting tax is always bad! In wanting the pupils to understand that inner belief and conviction shows in changed actions and lives she remembered a verse from somewhere in the Bible which reads, 'Faith without works is useless' (John 2:20). Perhaps she would discuss this verse with the pupils. She wondered about inviting a Christian in to talk about the difference their faith made to them and what they did. She thought that would be ok. Although she had a clear plan she wanted to remain flexible and incorporate ideas and questions from the pupils.

Finally, she planned an activity. In pairs, the pupils could imagine the conversation between Jesus and Zacchaeus at the meal table. They would then fill in some speech bubbles to show this developing dialogue and its outcome. At the end of the lesson, she could ask the pupils what sort of person they thought Jesus must have been to make Zacchaeus change like that. What would a Christian answer? She introduced the RE concept of the week – repentance – and wrote this on the wall. The pupils would add ideas around this word such as titles of relevant stories, poems and synonyms. She thought about what other stories the pupils might go on to consider about people who changed when they met Jesus and the difference this made. She had some great ideas for progression and noted them down before forgetting them.

On another day she filled a bowl with water, adding a couple of flowers and a floating candle. She reminded the pupils of the story and asked them to write something down on rice paper for which they were sorry and they floated the paper till it melted. The pupils were very reflective during this activity.

Task three: Using USER

Now work out the USER steps for one of the following: the stilling of the storm by Jesus, Christian Baptism, The concept of reconciliation, Advent.

- Unpack the material using the USER Strategy;
- Decide which two questions to ask the pupils about the material;
- Think of visual aids that might help you teach about the story or concept;
- Propose one follow-up activity that will reinforce the learning that does not entail the pupils doing any writing.

You can read more about Concept Cracking and see more examples of planned RE using this framework (http://www.stapleford-centre.org). It is worth remembering that you will never crack a concept 'once and for all'. A concept like forgiveness, or sin, or contentment: each could be studied for a lifetime, and with any luck the concept will 'spiral' up through a pupil's school career. Lesley Bull was eight when she wrote her poem. Here is a teenager writing about visiting a prayer space:

> There is a lot of times in especially teenage life where there's points where you can have a downfall and your parents can just let go and really get angry at you and the Prayer Space kind of helps you let go of everything and come into reality of I've done something wrong I need to apologise and it just helps you go home and face what you have done yes.
>
> (Stern and Shillitoe 2018, p 16)

Forgiveness develops throughout our lives, and teachers, too, may need to ask for forgiveness. Pupils certainly appreciate it if a teacher admits that they got something wrong – whether they told off the wrong pupil, they spent the whole day being grumpy, they said a pupil was incorrect when they were right, they were tough on a recently bereaved pupil or they borrowed an item from a pupil and forgot to return it. Because RE covers so many complex and sensitive issues, there are often times when a teacher will need to apologize. Your pupils will forgive you. What they won't forgive is you pretending you are perfect and never get anything wrong.

Seeing the big picture

Realizing that forgiveness and other concepts develop throughout our lives is part of seeing the 'big picture' in RE, and in life. Seeing the big picture is important, for a whole religious tradition as much as for an individual concept (Figure 3.10).

One big issue in teaching RE in primary school is how to provide pupils with a holistic view of a religion rather than a set of fragmented, unrelated parts. How can the teacher help the pupils gain a big picture of Christianity through teaching about

Figure 3.10 The big picture

the Bible, for example? One way might be to take a chronologically situated Bible story each week to show how the book is constructed and the stories relate to each other and build into one narrative. This does not need to be contained in the RE lesson. An idea to show how these narratives fit together might be to hang artefacts across the room on a washing line to reveal the story of the Bible. The first object might be a globe followed by a tree or an apple, an ark or rainbow, Father Abraham and his family, Joseph and his multicoloured coat, some bulrushes and so on. There are accompanying songs for some of these stories in pupils' songbooks or the inventive teacher may compose some.

As well as seeing how the stories fit together, the pupils can see how the Bible is constructed into two parts and includes different types of writings. This can be done by having a Bible colour-coded 'bookshelf' made from matchboxes with the Bible books written on the spine. A class was asked to identify the two parts of the Bible. A small girl raised her hand and said 'Part-fact and part-fiction'. Not quite the answer the teacher was expecting, but it led to interesting discussion about how some Christians maintain that all scripture is 'God-breathed' while others take a different view (Figure 3.11).

There are various ways that can help pupils build up a holistic picture of Christianity and two are introduced here.

The pedagogical ideas underpinning Concept Cracking have been central in the development of a substantial resource called *Understanding Christianity* (http://www.understandingchristianity.org.uk). The key purpose of this project is to help

Figure 3.11 Parts of the Bible

How the parts of the bible relate...

Old Testament and New Testament and...

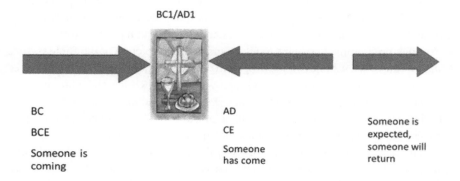

BC1/AD1

BC

BCE

Someone is
coming

AD

CE

Someone
has come

Someone is
expected,
someone will
return

all teachers support pupils in developing their thinking and understanding of Christianity, as a contribution to their understanding of the world and their own experience within it. Knowing how some non-specialist teachers of RE can flounder, the programme seeks to empower and support teachers in their own theological understanding. It contains and recommends resources for Early Years through to those for secondary RE. For example, the *Puddles and Freddie* series (e.g. Vaisey and Gwillym 2004) covers different aspects of Christian faith and experience, including harvest, Christmas, Easter, weddings, baptism and helping others.

The material deals with some big overarching aspects of Christian theology and revisits some of these across the years of primary education. The main concepts are God, Creation, Fall, People of God, Incarnation, Gospel, Salvation and the Kingdom of God, and the main aim of the resource is for pupils to 'leave school with a coherent understanding of Christian belief and practice' and to 'explore the significant theological concepts within Christianity as part of developing their wider religious, theological and cultural literacy' (http://www. understandingchristianity.org.uk). In this way, RE teaching about Christianity can be creative and can be respectful of Christian traditions and the beliefs of your pupils. Training is necessary to teach this programme and it costs to gain the resources, but many RE teachers and schools have taken advantage of this. *Understanding Christianity* aims

- to enable pupils to know about and understand Christianity as a living world faith, by exploring core theological concepts;

- to enable pupils to develop knowledge and skills in making sense of biblical texts and understanding their impact in the lives of Christians and

- to develop pupils' abilities to connect, critically reflect upon, evaluate and apply their learning to their own growing understanding of religion and belief (particularly Christianity), of themselves, the world and human experience (http://www.understandingchristianity.org.uk).

By addressing three questions in each of the designed units the material helps pupils understand how they can make sense of the biblical texts; the possible impact of these texts on Christians' beliefs and actions and the possible connections between the texts and concepts and the pupils' own lives and understanding of the world.

Another programme that helps pupils to grasp the big picture of the Bible is *Bible Explorer* (http://www.bible.org.uk/wtb_child_events.php); although this is designed for Christian nurture and so should be used with care in RE lessons, you may have seen this being taught in school. The *Understanding Christianity* and *Bible Explorer* materials are produced by or for Christian organizations. There will be other perspectives on what Christianity means, from other Christian and non-Christian groups. It is important that, as a teacher of RE, you recognize the perspectives of the people who produce the material you use. After all, that is what RE teaching always involves: trying to understand different people. But you should be careful to avoid treating one perspective as always right when you are teaching pupils, as that will mean telling pupils with different religions or non-religious views that they are wrong. You will have your own views, of course: it is just that you should be able to say 'some Christians believe that …', or 'many Sikhs do this …', rather than saying 'Christians all believe this, and this is true'.

Being creative is a disciplined process

All the descriptions of creativity presented in this chapter are *disciplined* approaches. Creativity in general does not mean 'anything goes'. Artists, musicians, actors, poets and dancers, all will say that being creative is itself a *discipline*. In RE, therefore, being creative does not simply mean inventing things and saying what we like about religious or other worldviews. Inventing a 'modern' set of ten commandments may be a worthwhile activity, and may encourage some creativity, but if it means that the pupils fail to understand the significance of the biblical commandments, then the creativity will be a *distraction* from good RE. Why not, instead, ask older pupils to study the biblical commandments, and then watch television soap operas or pupils' news programmes (or read well-established news websites) and list which commandments are broken by which characters/people? If the use of music in RE lessons is restricted to the occasional chart hit that mentions an RE topic, the pupils will be distracted from the wealth of religious music (from every religious and non-religious tradition) that is important to those traditions. A simple search for 'Christian music' on YouTube will generate a fine starting point. (For a contrast, a search for 'Humanist music' will also generate plenty of ideas.)

Lat Blaylock set up and continues to support *Spirited Arts* (http://www.natre.org.uk/about-natre/projects/spirited-arts/) and we have used several images from the site in this book. Thousands of pupils contribute their art on a specific theme each year, with 25,000 contributing on the theme of 'art in heaven', for example. This work can promote the understanding of religious and non-religious traditions ('learning about religion'), and it can also promote learning *from* those traditions. Why not visit the Gallery online? Religious art from across the centuries is very easily available (e.g. from images.google.com), and Blaylock suggests exploring contemporary art, too, in order to help pupils understand the religious tradition that they – in their own work – can contribute to with their own art. Paintings by Lewis Lavoie (http://www.muralmosaic.com/), who constructs large paintings out of many smaller paintings, are good to stimulate pupils' thoughts about vital topics in RE. His *Adam*, a version of Michelangelo's Sistine Chapel Adam, is made up of people of the world, and refers to the United Nations. The idea of the biblical Adam being a person of and for the whole world is explored through this work of art. Pupils are entranced by watching the video on the artist's website of him painting the elements that go to make up *Adam*. It is not difficult to see how pupils would follow this up with a theme of their own.

In these and many more ways, RE can and should be creative and disciplined *at the same time*.

Pause for thought

Find out what this year's themes are for the NATRE *spirited arts* competition.

- Work out which theme would suit an issue in teaching Christianity that you have found challenging (from all the issues mentioned in this chapter).
- Write a lesson for your pupils that would introduce that issue, and the possibility of entering the spirited arts competition.
- Work out a way of assessing the pupils' work, according to how well it demonstrates their learning *about* Christianity, and how well it demonstrates what they have learned *from* Christianity.
- Propose one follow-up activity that will reinforce the learning that does not entail the pupils doing any writing.

Summary

So, in a chapter that has been primarily concerned with ways to teach about and from Christianity as a world religion, we have encouraged you to find time to question normative ways of teaching Christianity that you may have experienced. In developing creative ways of teaching that help to maintain and develop pupils' curiosity, your own creativity will be developed as an innovative teacher. Perhaps you might adapt some of the principles of Godly Play for the classroom or encourage the pupils you work with to enter the Spirited Arts competition. Or perhaps you might develop a throng of angels for the Christmas display in the hall and consider what their messages of encouragement might be to the world. Dare we mention fun and enjoyment in learning in RE? We do hope so.

Recommended reading

Cooling, T (1994) *Concept Cracking: Exploring Christian Beliefs in School*; Stapleford, Nottinghamshire: The Stapleford Centre (also available online at http://www.staplefordcentre.org/).

Office for Standards in Education (Ofsted) (2013) *Religious Education: Realising the Potential*; Manchester: Ofsted (also available online at http://www.ofsted.gov.uk/resources/religious-education-realising-potential).

Chapter 4
Religious Education as a Practical Activity

Chapter objectives

- What counts as practical activity in RE?
- Why should RE be a practical activity?
- Teaching and learning in practical ways in RE
  - Taking visits and learning outdoors
  - Celebrating visitors
  - Handling artefacts
  - Naturally speaking
  - Getting arty

Introduction

In this chapter we consider practical ways to teach RE. In order to do this, we discern what counts as legitimate practical activity in the subject, what could be tricky and what is not appropriate. Looking at various ways already used in many schools might give you confidence to plan more innovative lessons – such as taking the pupils outdoors or inviting people to talk to the pupils about their religion and worldview. In using art as an exemplar for cross-curricular work in RE, we hope that you will be encouraged to seek ways of making links with other curriculum subjects and thus break free from the constraints of a divided curriculum. We maintain that this is a positive and exciting way to learn.

What counts as practical activity in RE?

Have you noticed how many people praise children as being good because they sit still and keep quiet? Why is this? Young children are active beings, so engaging with religions and worldviews in active and engaging ways makes common sense in the primary school. In practical activities, the youngest pupils use their senses to explore and the learning can become real, affective and memorable. Religions have called on people to use their senses for millennia. Consider, for example, the Eucharist of Christianity where all five senses are employed in active participative learning, and the puja ceremony in Hinduism. Think of other examples and how you might teach RE in sensory ways. You might list the five senses and list different ways of appealing to each of the senses in RE. For example, hearing a bell, a pebble dropped into water, a door closing or opening, running water, the sound of fire. And perhaps the sound of one hand clapping? (See Chapter 7, and Olson 2005 or Stern 2007, pp 88–9.)

What counts as effective practical activity in RE? It does not include coercing pupils to act in quasi-religious ways, mimicking ritual and behaviours that are central to the way believers practice. From observation and experience in schools, the following appear to be some of the most common forms of facilitating practical RE: visits to places of worship, inviting visitors in to talk with (rather than at) the pupils, handling artefacts, making food appropriate to a tradition, dressing up, drama, painting, sculpting, music-making and the like. These ways are productive for RE, as long as the integrity of the specific RE material is retained and does not become subsumed or forgotten in and through the activity.

Task one: Practical RE

- Make a list of as many practical activities that you have seen in school.
- Think about how you might utilize these in active ways of learning in RE.
- Are there some activities that would not be appropriate in RE? Why?

This chapter looks at practical activity in RE through visits and visitors, artefacts, the natural world and art.

Why should RE be a practical activity?

RE should be a practical activity so as to avoid passive learning methodologies. Primary aged pupils learn best about abstract concepts such as worship, faith and commitment when they encounter them in real terms. The best religion and belief systems are essentially active too: dogma and theology that stay static and ineffective remain abstract; it is when religious teachings and wisdom become practical and useful through their enactment, they become effective for making sense of life and living.

There are many educational theorists who support practical activity for learning. What follows here is a brief mention of a few educational theorists who have impacted on present educational thinking, and assumptions are drawn of how their theories might support practical teaching and learning in RE. You might like to think about others that you know and how they might do likewise. Introductory texts to seminal theorists written by Pound (2009) and Palmer (2001) are recommended to support this chapter or you might visit http://infed.org/mobi/category/thinkers-and-innovators/

- Froebel (1782–1852) encouraged teachers to begin from where the learner is and as pupils are naturally inquisitive, curious and active, devising practical ways to learn is a good starting place. He saw play as vital for pupils' development and stressed that they should have first-hand experience of beauty and nature in the world. For Froebel, developing the spiritual in all things was important and he maintained that space and light are important factors in facilitating learning environments. Presumably, Froebel would have supported the notion of learning outside of the classroom through taking pupils on visits to places of worship. It can be surmised that he would have endorsed a pedagogy that facilitates space where the mind can play, calling for creative and non-didactic methods of teaching and learning.

- Dewey (1859–1952) supported the theory that children learn best in real-life situations. He believed education is actual living not a preparation for future living, so the teacher's role is to help children live in society and to learn to shape that society. Social learning cannot be developed merely sitting at a desk using competitive and combative modes of learning. Dewey maintained that children are like scientists and scientists grow their theories out of practices, so children need to engage in activities and experiences that contribute to their understanding of the world. Such learning can become cross-curricular outside of the confines of the somewhat arbitrary boundaries of the curriculum. Dewey would have supported the social aspects of learning in RE.

- Montessori (1870–1952) maintained that children learn best through movement and through the senses. She understood that they have 'sensitive periods' when they are more inclined to learn about new ideas. Daily living and social development were at the centre of her ideas, while creating opportunity for care of the environment, oneself and others in the community was especially important for the child's development. Her curriculum and the Montessori method aim to provide experience of the natural world, people, events and cultures. Presumably she would have advocated children studying how those with faith and worldviews seek to protect and care for others and the environment.

- Vygotsky (1896–1934) emphasized the role that language plays in a child's development of thought and their social and cultural learning. He believed that this development is part of and results from social interaction between the pupils themselves and the pupil with teachers and others. In his theory of the Zone of Proximal Development, the child's interaction with a more knowledgeable other is crucial to their ongoing development. Vygotsky stressed the way that knowledge and understanding are constructed by the learner from their experiences. Welcoming visitors into the school so children might dialogue with members of faith groups and with those holding different worldviews would have been a popular strategy with him. Vygotsky would have championed a pedagogy and culture of dialogue in the classroom.

- Bruner (1915–2016) saw the child as active learner and problem-solver who strives to make sense of the world and their place within it. He introduced the spiral curriculum in the 1960s and felt that any subject might be taught effectively in an intellectual and honest way to children at any stage of their development. Bruner's three stages or modes – the enactive, iconic and symbolic modes – are not linear but correlate to the need for the child to be active, learning how to use one thing to represent another and to be adept at representing experience through a range of symbolic systems. He appreciated the place of culture in shaping the mind and helping the child to construct their world and their own identity. So, in line with his three modes, Bruner would be supportive of practical learning through the child playing, building, painting, acting and investigating the cultural and ritualistic manifestations of religion. He would support children appreciating language in new ways, and so presumably, that used by faith groups in their revered writings.

These are just a few theorists who advocate practical activity to aid the pupil's social, cultural, spiritual, linguistic and intellectual development. Theories, however, remain ineffective if their impact is not realized in practice, so discover some other educational theories and the implications they have for practical teaching and learning in RE.

Teaching and learning in practical ways in RE

Taking visits and learning outdoors

Learning outside the classroom through taking visits makes learning relevant to real-life contexts away from the confines of classroom-based learning. Direct encounters with the natural world and real people's lives can reinvigorate learning, by turning abstract learning into concrete experiences. In these encounters, pupils can begin to ask questions and seek to find the answers, acting as detectives. Imagine taking pupils on a visit to a traditional Anglican church. A good question to start with might be 'who meets here and why?' As Hudson shows 'Any place of worship will contain a vast range of overt and hidden symbolic material revealing much about the beliefs and practices of those who worship there, or who have worshipped there in the past' (http://www.rethinking.co.uk). The history of the place might be seen in its sculpture and artwork, architecture and the overall layout of the building, and this may have changed over the years. Often the outside of the building can reveal much about the worshipping community and the religion. Through developing a pedagogy of question that will help pupils appreciate deeper meaning and significance, questions to pose might be the following:

- Why is the baptismal font near the entrance?
- Why is the lectern in the centre of the church?
- If we had a bird's-eye view of the church what would we see?
- Why did people create stained glass windows?

The history educator John Fines describes dozens of questions to set pupils going on a visit to a church or other site. One of his techniques was to say this:

> I am an old fat man, I can't gallop around anymore, can you find something really interesting to take me to see? Mind you, it must be interesting, because I don't want to get all out of breath going to see nothing at all.
>
> (Fines and Nichol 1997, p 231)

You might like to devise some other questions that would motivate the pupils to discover.

Planning for before, during and after the visit is vital to facilitate good educational experiences. Pupils need access to specific vocabulary, so they can express their new learning. However, no matter how well the teacher plans, the unexpected often happens as the following true (but anonymized) story testifies:

> A class of six-year-old pupils visit an Anglican church after learning about the roles of the workers. A curious and high-spirited girl, Jennifer, is greeted by a rather stern-faced church worker expecting the highest standards of behaviour from the pupils. Imagine, if you will, Jennifer approaching the worker (whom we shall call Miss Jones) shouting out excitedly 'I know who you are, you are the Virgin Miss Jones!'. So much for the introduction and correct use of ecclesiastical vocabulary. One verger remained unimpressed!

So often on visits, pupils notice the small details and make much of them. The attentive teacher will take these and use them to elicit good learning opportunities. Watson and Thompson recall an example of a child who visits a church and chooses to draw the electric wires emerging from the electricity box, rather than something that might have been thought to be more RE relevant by the well-planned teacher. In this example, the teacher asks the child why the church needs electricity, focusing on the microphone to the pulpit and then proceeds to ask if there is electricity, why are candlesticks there if not to supply light to the church (Watson and Thompson 2006, p 35). The temptation might have been for the teacher to say 'Okay, but come and look at …'. It may well be the homeless person whom the pupils notice on one visit that leads to a discussion and exploration of how those from religious and other worldviews seek to help others and be involved in charities.

Which questions would you ask pupils on a visit to the local mosque? What questions would help them link place, worship, celebration and community? How could you prepare pupils and their parents for such a visit? Find out how the community celebrates in the place of worship and at home.

Sayad (aged eight) links the mosque with celebration in the following (Figure 4.1):

Eid Mubarak

Eid is the festival at the end of the 28 days of fasting in Ramadan. The is a watercolour painting of Eid. I hope you have noticed how I have tried to blend the colours orange, blue and purple. My main ideas were to blend the colours.

My picture shows people going to the mosque in the morning. At the mosque people pray to Allah. After we pray we go home and eat delicious food. We also wear special clothes. Eid Mubarak: it means 'Happy Festival'.

These pupils developed a display about the role of the mosque (Figure 4.2).

Figure 4.1 Eid, by Syad

Figure 4.2 The Mosque, by Our Lady Queen of Martyrs RC Primary School, York

Task two: A visit

Consider taking a Year 5 class on a visit to a Hindu mandir and work through the stages of planning and completing the tasks listed below. If your own knowledge and understanding about the mandir and its place in Hindu worship is insecure, then some research will be necessary. You should visit a mandir before completing this task: a pre-visit is essential before any trip and is a good way of finding out what will be expected of visitors. Investigate whether the school or local SACRE have guidance about taking visits to places of worship. These visits encourage a greater understanding of important relationships such as those between beliefs and practice, culture and religion, community and religious life.

- To begin planning, write four reasons why you think visits to places of worship are educationally valuable.
- Consider what you might write in a letter sent to parents to justify the visit.
- Think about how you would respond to a parent who might have misgivings about such a visit.
- What could you include in an evening's presentation where teaching colleagues presented a session on 'Visits to Religious Buildings' for parents?

Before the visit consider the following:

- How you will equip the pupils with a working vocabulary for what they will encounter, and what key **concepts** do you need to introduce or develop further?
- How you might use guidance on trips from websites such as http://www.reonline.org.uk/?
- Would a preliminary virtual tour by the pupils be useful?

Have you ever witnessed hordes of pupils at places of worship or museums laden with sheets containing numerous activities to complete? Often, in religious buildings, it is best to let the pupils dwell in the place in order to stop and ponder. Some pupils will not have experienced such an imposing place before. At some point space will be needed for the pupils to compile a list of *their* questions that they want to investigate. Cameras, if allowed, are a good way to capture images of the place which can then be annotated and discussed back in the classroom. For young pupils, Teddy placed in a significant place with a well-expressed question card (e.g. 'Teddy wonders what happens here, and why?') will help the pupils learn.

During the visit, think about the following:

- Who will speak to the pupils and about what?
- Whether you will brief the speaker in some way.
- Where the time for quiet and reflection will occur?
- The overall focus of the visit, enabling deep rather than shallow learning.
- What **attitudes** you want the pupils to develop, further, during the experience.

Will the visit include the following?

- Involvement in showing practical ways of respect.
- Appreciation that communities contribute to society and how different traditions exist in the same religion.
- Developing greater curiosity through 'hands on' experience.
- Understanding and empathy through dialogue with members of the faith community.

How might the following **skills** be developed?

- observation, investigation and imagination;
- enquiry through asking questions, listening and communicating using appropriate language;
- appreciation that there are many different means of expression in religion and the ability to understand the synthesis of inner belief and outer action;
- interpretation through reading the symbolism in architecture, ritual and religious art.

What will the pupils do in the place? Here are a few ideas, to which you can add some of your own.

- Just sitting still, closed eyes and feeling the place, then writing three words that sum up the experience.
- Meeting a believer/worker and asking them questions.
- Hunting the symbol: going on a symbol trail.
- Discovering by reading the notice boards and epitaphs.
- Taking photos of anything interesting or different.
- Finding things that make you happy, sad, peaceful.
- Discovering a bird, animal, flower, something red.
- Finding something that tells you this is a place for Hindus (or Sikhs, or Christians or so on).
- Finding out about someone who is named in the building.
- Discovering how music is used in this place.
- Writing down three questions that come to mind.

After the visit, look at the following and discern the educational scope of each of the activities for the pupils' cognitive, conceptual and skill development in RE.

- Develop a guidebook, floor plan or model for the place of worship for a younger class.
- Develop a virtual guide with voice-overs and images.
- Look at the words and meanings of sacred songs used in the place and compose a piece of music for use in the place.

- Consider how the religious community might spend a donation of £100,000.
- Interview a worker and produce 'a day in the life of ...' the worker, and write a job description too.
- Find out about the community links and design a new club, meeting or service for a group that meets there and think about how this might be advertised to the community.
- Design a new place for reflection and/or worship for the community.
- Write a letter or post a blog to say thank you to the community, noting what amazed, surprised, reminded, intrigued or saddened you.
- Design a stained glass window or an artefact that reinforces an aspect of belief, a painting to be hung or an annex to the building (Figures 4.3 and 4.4).

Hookway (http://www.rethinking.co.uk) has devised a grid for helping older pupils interpret actions and artefacts found in places of worship according to different viewpoints. The chart below is based on her idea. She uses a font, pulpit/lectern, altar, cross/crucifix and candles for a church, and the act of washing, a shoe rack, the mihrab and calligraphy for a mosque. You might like to devise sheets for the gurdwara, mosque, synagogue, mandir and Buddhist temple. The grid could be completed individually or as a group and an image added in the first section.

Figure 4.3 Faith window 1, by Year 4 pupils from St Peter's CE Primary School, Farnham

Figure 4.4 Faith window 2, by Year 4 pupils from St Peter's CE Primary School, Farnham

An Anglican Church	When a Christian sees a ... he/she might learn / think	When a member of another religion sees ... he/she might learn/think	When an atheist sees ... he/she might learn/ think	What I learn/ think
A font	Water is used in baptism and reminds me of being washed from wrongdoing, sin.	Christians use water as a sign of becoming clean and being forgiven.	Water can remind us of being refreshed.	
The altar	It is important not to forget that Jesus died and rose again.	It was bad that Jesus was crucified, but this shows that some great people are prepared to sacrifice themselves for others.	Jesus might have existed and was a good man. His death was a tragedy, and it shows the importance of self-sacrifice.	
Candles				

Learning outside in RE does not need to be restricted to visiting places of worship. Hudson (http://www.rethinking.co.uk) suggests interesting ways to problem-solve in the environment. He uses the idea of designing and building a Jewish sukkah from natural materials and sharing a meal within. Sukkahs are constructed during the annual Jewish festival of Sukkot when some Jews build outdoor shelters to remember the Exodus story of their ancestors as desert nomads and their dependence on Yahweh who provided for them. Hudson proposes, 'afterwards, reflect on how aspects of a re-enactment "connect" participants with the collective memory of an original event' (http://www.rethinking.co.uk). This activity could be a class project to build a sukkah outdoors, but pupils might prepare for this in the classroom by making models from small boxes, leaving gaps in the roofing so that the sky and stars can be seen. The pupils might design an appropriate meal using kosher laws for food and make cards with Jewish symbols on them to invite others. Sitting in the sukkah, they could creatively recall why Jews acknowledge Sukkot. In one university, student teachers built a sukkah in their grounds and invited staff and fellow students to share a meal in the shelter. As an adult, sitting within this temporary structure and eating food with others while being reminded of the account of the wandering Jewish people makes this experience truly memorable. Find some images of some sukkahs from around the world on https://images.google.com/ and share them with the pupils, asking them where they like to share food with others and why.

Celebrating visitors

There are many people of faith and worldview who will be happy to visit and speak to the pupils. SACREs can often advise schools on appropriate people or groups. It is important that such visitors understand the reason for the visit. It is also wise to prime pupils for visitors by preparing questions that they might ask. But often, the best dialogue is impromptu and improvised as the relationship between guest and pupils develops. It takes courage to trust in this process, but this is where the richest conversations can take place. However, a few planned preliminary questions might be helpful so that the visitor's pet or favourite colour does not become the focus of the conversation. A wise guest, if reminded of the age and aptitude of the pupils, might bring in artefacts, photographs, videos or other items of interest.

CASE STUDY: A visitor

A vicar comes to speak to a Year 3 class. He brings a suitcase and the pupils are amazed that the first thing he withdraws is a nappy. This man also takes out a cup and saucer, communion set, a Bible, computer keypad and a chasuble among other vocational and daily items. The pupils have to guess why these items are important to him and this leads to him outlining 'One day in the life of a vicar' using the artefacts as prompts and showing a video of his day. The vicar uses humour to great effect, a vital tool in teaching. The teacher goes on to invite a rabbi and imam to talk to the pupils on the same theme.

Handling artefacts

Even a simple table of artefacts such as this one for the Jewish Shabbat will intrigue the pupils as they enter the classroom. Add music and different lighting and the mood is set for learning (Figure 4.5).

Artefacts can help pupils piece together a picture of faith. Many trainee teachers note how exciting they find engagement with artefacts for their own learning. One student wrote, 'I look forward to RE, principally because I never know what is going to be waiting for us on the table'. Most schools have a box of artefacts for each religion compiled by the RE coordinator and some generous parents.

Figure 4.5 Shabbat table

Task three: Artefacts

Research the following artefacts and their use in the lives of believers. Add two more to each list.

Buddhism – a prayer wheel, stupa (thupa/cetiya), mandala.

Christianity – paschal candle, fish brooch, rosary.

Hinduism – murti of Ganesh, puja tray, diva lamp.

Islam – topi, subhah, qibla.

Judaism – tallit, Havdalah candle, hanukkiah

Sikhism – Chauri, Nishan Sahib, kangha.

A good pattern for working with artefacts is offered by Logan (1998). He suggests that there are five levels of understanding to develop and the following is based on his ideas.

Level one: Observational level

- What does the artefact look like?
- What are its different features?
- Use your senses to examine the object.

The youngest pupils can engage with an artefact at this level, as developed writing skills are not necessary. The teacher might begin with a feely box or bag to arouse curiosity. The teacher might introduce questions such as 'do you have/use anything that is a bit like this?' and 'what does this remind you of?', building bridges between the familiar and the new. With young pupils, some of these artefacts may be used in the home corner as special objects that help the pupils develop understanding of their use. Examples are given later in this chapter.

Level two: Investigational level

- What is it?
- What is it used for?
- What group of people uses it?

Again, all pupils can interact with the artefacts at this level. Some may be able to write questions for investigation, or an adult can scribe the questions. This method of enquiry will motivate the pupils for the next stage.

Level three: Contextual level

How does the artefact fit into

- the life of the believer,

- the worship of the believer and
- the faith of the believer?

The teacher can introduce effective resources at this stage to help the pupils connect the object to the life, practice and belief of the believer/follower. An effective way is for someone to talk from a faith perspective about the artefact, or for the pupils to visit a place where the object is being used. If this is not feasible, then photocards, video clips, the web and picture books will all help the child understand the meaning and use of the object and thus, its deeper significance. You might like to find out about 'A Gift to the Child' project and materials at this point (Grimmitt et al. 1991), and how the programme uses artefacts in a phenomenological way to teach RE.

Level four: Reflective level

- At this level, pupils appreciate the deeper significance and symbolism of the object, and may discover links between the artefact and their own lives and experiences.

Level five: Devotional level

This is the final level noted by Logan and is not the remit of the school but the domain of the faith community and home. This level refers to the use of the artefact in worship and devotion and moves the outsider to an insider encounter. Pupils should not be asked to use the prayer mat to join in with the Muslim practice of rakah – a part of the ritual bows and prostrations of salat, the prescribed prayers said five times a day. They will not drink grape juice and eat bread in a simulated Eucharist. These practices are to be respected and seen as sacred aspects of belief and practice to be expressed by the committed. The line between what is permissible or wise and what is not, in RE, can be difficult to understand, but the RE coordinator in the school will help with the complexities, and SACREs and other bodies often offer guidance.

Task four: A mezuzah

This task involves using an artefact to teach about Jewish belief and practice. The following object is a picture of a Jewish mezuzah that holds a small paper scroll containing the Shema – words from Deuteronomy, a book in the Jewish Torah and Christian Bible (Figures 4.6 and 4.7).

Investigate

- how a Jew will use this object and its importance in Jewish life and worship,
- why these words called the Shema (translation from the Hebrew is included above) are important for Jews,
- ways a Jew might take these words literally through what they wear and do.

Figure 4.6 Shema

A Jewish mezuzah

Shema

Figure 4.7 Deuteronomy 6

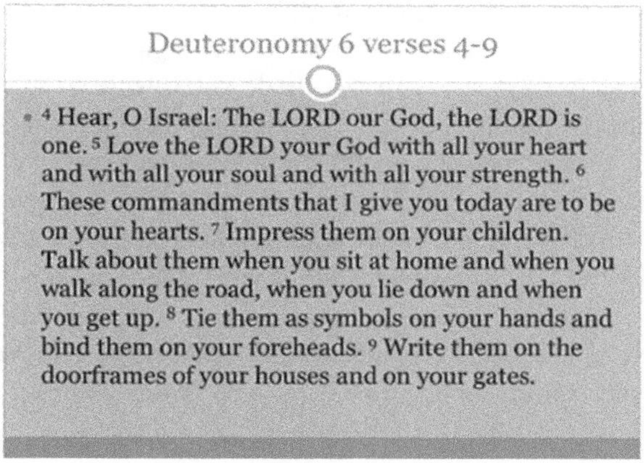

> Deuteronomy 6 verses 4-9
>
> 4 Hear, O Israel: The LORD our God, the LORD is one. 5 Love the LORD your God with all your heart and with all your soul and with all your strength. 6 These commandments that I give you today are to be on your hearts. 7 Impress them on your children. Talk about them when you sit at home and when you walk along the road, when you lie down and when you get up. 8 Tie them as symbols on your hands and bind them on your foreheads. 9 Write them on the doorframes of your houses and on your gates.

Imagine that you are to teach a Year 3 class about the mezuzah. Write two learning objectives for the lesson. Ensure that these focus on learning about the specific Jewish practice and its deeper meaning, while making links with the pupils' lives and experiences of the world. The learning objectives might begin with the following:

- To be able to recognize …
- To be able to …
- To know that …
- To understand …
- To be able to reflect on …

Consider how you would introduce the artefact to the class, teach about it and design an activity that would help the pupils learn about and reflect on the material. You might choose as foci special words; a special object; obedience to God's commandments; signs of belonging.

One student teacher asked the pupils to make nets for a cuboid. They then decorated their containers with symbols that were personally significant and made a small scroll to put inside, containing their special words. These were then put around the doorframe of the classroom to show that the pupils belonged to the class community.

The last sentence of the Shema is the mitzvah (commandment) of the mezuzah. Another teacher asked the pupils to design a mezuzah cover to be given as a present to a Jewish family and their new home. This must be able to hold the script; it must be weatherproof, and should be able to be attached and removed to the doorpost and decorated with Jewish symbols or stories.

Bearing in mind Logan's fifth level of using artefacts (the 'devotional level'), consider whether you think that these activities were appropriate. Why or why not?

Artefacts may be used to introduce a festival, ritual or belief. One way into the study of the Jewish festival of Hanukkah might be to play a game of dreidel that is often enjoyed at this time. It is a minor festival in the Jewish calendar, and should not dominate RE: the game that follows is more popular with, and familiar to, RE teachers than to Jewish children in many parts of the world. Nevertheless, it makes for a good activity and – along with the other festivals mentioned in this book – is still well worth a go. It involves playing dreidels or, if you have not got dreidels, cut a small square card and write the Jewish letters along each side. Spin the dreidel and play the game.

Ask the pupils to investigate the game's significance in the context of the festival. There are different interpretations of the game, and of the letters on the sides of the dreidel (Figure 4.8).

Figure 4.8 Dreidel (taken from http://www.myjewishlearning.com)

Rules of the game

Each player has a kitty of counters or chocolates. (Money is sometimes used, but this would not be appropriate in the classroom.)

Each player puts one coin or counter in the middle.

The pupils take turns in spinning the dreidel and obey the rules below according to how the dreidel falls.

Shin = puts one in the centre   Hey = take half
Gimel = take all   Nun = do nothing

Every time there are no counters or coins in the middle, each person must add one so that the kitty is sustained. A dreidel song can be sung:

I have a little dreidel
I made it out of clay
And when it's dry and ready
Then dreidel I shall play
Oh dreidel, dreidel, dreidel,
I made it out of clay
And when it's dry and ready
Then dreidel I shall play

https://www.youtube.com/watch?v=TwV1TZtdaKw

The pupils might proceed to find out about other aspects of the Hanukkah festival and their deeper significance for Jews.

Task five: More festivals

Investigate one other Jewish festival according to the following components, used in Chapter 3, and consider how you might use an artefact (not necessarily an explicitly religious article) to introduce

- the story/account behind the festival,
- the customs and traditions associated with it,
- the inner belief behind the festival,
- the experience of a contemporary child from that tradition.

Some themes of the Hanukkah festival are light, miracle, salvation/redemption and re-dedication. Choose a festival from the list below to research. Consider their associated main concepts and how you might teach about these at Key Stage 1 and build on the learning at Key Stage 2.

- Shabbat – rest, family, community, service.
- Passover – slavery, freedom, provision.

- Sukkot – remembering, harvest, provision, relationship.
- Purim – persecution, salvation/redemption, protection, identity.
- Simchat Torah – rejoicing in the Torah, law.
- Rosh Hashanah – sacrifice, new beginnings.
- Yom Kippur – forgiveness, atonement, scapegoat.

The two Jewish festivals of Shabbat and Simchat Torah are well suited for the Early Years. McCreery et al. (2008) understand young pupils' love for fantasy and need for play as a gift. The imaginative teacher can create play spaces where they can encounter religious meaning through play and the use of story. However, they warn that the pupils' language and experience acquisition will not always allow them to access explicitly religious concepts, so it is often good to introduce these through the life of a child from the tradition. It is important to weave RE into the Early Years areas of learning which offer rich contexts for such learning.

The concept of 'special' instead of 'holy' or 'sacred' will be helpful with young pupils in terms of objects, names, people, places, books, days and times. To begin a topic on 'Special Places', the pupils might begin by bringing in a picture of their special place and how they feel when they are there. The teacher might introduce special places in story time. So, Plop the owlet's story (Tomlinson and Howard 2002) could be shared, and the pupils might discuss where his special place is and how he can be afraid when not there. Together, they might create a special place for a doll or imaginary character and investigate the theme further. The teacher might discuss what is in this place, what colours, sounds and feelings might be associated with it, who might enter and the like. Having looked at their own special place they could begin to identify those in the locale, and other people's special places, and lead on to looking at special places of worship where people might be able to stop and think.

A colleague who teaches RE at Winchester University takes her student teachers outdoors to consider this theme. Rhiannon and her colleagues are committed to developing a slow pedagogy in RE that includes pausing, peering and pondering. She writes the following (Figures 4.9 and 4.10):

Honoré (2004) in his book *In Praise of Slow* reports that a growing body of evidence suggests pupils learn better at a slower pace, resulting in pupils who are not only less anxious, but also importantly demonstrate an increased eagerness to learn as well as the ability to think independently. This is a challenge in today's educational climate where there can be pressure towards what Payne and Wattchow (2009) call a 'fast, take-away, virtual, globalized, download/uptake version of pedagogy'. This is particularly a concern with the curriculum subject of RE. The subtleties and complexities involved in learning about living faiths and traditions necessitates, in my view, a different approach, a slower pedagogy.

This belief led to my involvement in a collaborative learning experience of 'Awe-full Education' where we took second year BEd primary languages, geography and RE subject specialists into the woods to make time to 'Pause, Peer and Ponder' (Love, Seymour and Witt, quoted in Pickering 2017, p 64). Through this session we hoped that students would slow down, connect with the outdoors and see learning with a new perspective, as well as to build relationships with each other.

The afternoon consisted of a range of activities and adventures in the woods: making stick families after reading *Monsieur Bout-de-Bois* – the French version of Julia Donaldson's *Stick Man* (Donaldson and Scheffler 2008), making leaf people after reading *Leaf Man* by Lois Ehlert (2005), creating 'special places' for our stick families, before creating dens or 'special places' for themselves – all of the time encouraging the students to consider connections to concepts such as special, sacred, place, etc., that are central in RE.

We discussed with the students the idea of different perspectives – of seeing life, traditions, beliefs, etc., from a different point of view from their own – and to demonstrate this, they walked through the woods, looking at the view in mirrors held beneath their noses, which mimics the view that animals such as mice have of the world.

To conclude the afternoon, I led the students in a guided meditation. I was particularly keen to encourage the students to consider how important it is for children to have time to be quiet, to reflect and 'pause' in our hectic school days. This mediation evoked very mixed responses, with some students enthusiastic about stopping and being in the moment, while for some the quietness and inaction proved challenging.

Figure 4.9 A stick baby, by students at the University of Winchester

Figure 4.10 A special place for the stick family, by students at the University of Winchester

For young pupils, structured play where pupils might pause and ponder might mean making the Wendy house into a special place or a doll's house might have extra artefacts introduced. Think of various items that you might put in the home of a Jewish, Hindu, Christian or Sikh child – and let the pupils and their families help you. McCreery et al. give the example of setting up the home corner as Uzmah's home. Uzmah's family are Muslim. McCreery et al. suggest putting a cardboard copy of Uzmah at the entrance of the home, wearing a shalwar-kameez. Inside the home corner objects such as an Islamic calendar, Qur'an stand, wall decorations, prayer mat and prayer times, Eid cards, bowls of fruit and dates, zakat box, chapattis, a dressing up box, reading materials such as holiday destinations and books by the child's bed might be introduced (McCreery et al. 2008, pp 90–1). In addition, music could be introduced, along with photocards and a video. Uzmah might be taped, talking about her life at home and in the mosque. The pupils could imagine what they would talk about with Uzmah if they were to meet her or what they might want to find out.

Teachers might like to use persona dolls with young pupils. These are dolls dressed in cultural clothes from different traditions and they may have artefacts from particular religious perspectives. The doll can sit with the teacher and pupils and questions asked about what they do and believe following a short introduction from the teacher. The doll might have a photograph album or share their favourite story or verse with the pupils or speak about their special day of the week. How else might you use the doll? (See http://personadoll.uk/).

Task six: Home corners

Consider how you might set up the home corner for the following:

- Gurdeep's home.
- Ben and Rachel's home at Passover.
- The Christmas Stable.
- Anish's house at Diwali.
- Your own idea.

Naturally speaking

Like Rhiannon did with her student teachers, you might like to use a natural object to develop knowledge and understanding across a range of religions. One activity that Hudson (http://www.rethinking.co.uk) suggests for an outside context and an introduction to religious material is asking pupils to collect stones and pebbles and to study them. The links that can be made between the natural and sacred can surprise pupils and as good teaching often encompasses the surprising, this can be particularly effective. Stones often appear in religion and belief. Think about the mystical construction of Stonehenge. A stone is used in the Christian allegory, *The Lion the Witch and the Wardrobe* (Lewis 2000), the stone on which Aslan is killed. This stone splits at the time of his resurrection, reminiscent of the way Christians believe the stone was rolled away at Christ's resurrection or the temple curtain tore at his crucifixion. Christians and Jews speak of God in terms of being a rock. Pupils might consider what they believe Christians and Jews mean by this metaphor, and pupils may go on to develop their own ideas of what the metaphor might mean.

Hudson develops ideas about the humble stone to stimulate learning about different religions and worldviews (http://www.rethinking.co.uk). Some of his ideas are included below, while others have been added.

- 'Christians are said to be 'living stones'. Why? What are they building? Why did Jesus call Peter a rock?
- Jesus was called a 'keystone', as used to support an arch or bridge. Why?
- Muslims use the Black Stone and Ka'aba as a focus for worship at Makkah. Why?
- Jews remember how Jacob marked the place of God's revelation to him with a stone. Why?
- In the Torah, the people raised an Ebenezer (stone of help) to mark God's dealings with the people. Why?
- Zen Buddhists use small stones to create meditation gardens. In what other ways might stones be used by people?

Look at how McLean Bible Church in Washington, United States, has used this Ebenezer to celebrate what the community has achieved in establishing a church in the community, starting with the vision in 1961 of five families to worship God. This is just one of the stones charting the achievement that lead up to the entrance of the Church. The Church now holds many services each Sunday with thousands attending each one (Figure 4.11).

Using stones as a focus brings together what is shared in religious ideas and helps to make connections between ideas which can prove to be creative for teachers and learners. Pupils could use clay and many other materials to create their own monuments to mark some time or event in their own lives and explore monuments and statues in the locale to see who or what is remembered.

Practical and creative teachers keep abreast of the latest 'craze' and exploit the ideas.

While we write this book the craze for fidget spinners has diminished slightly and been replaced by painting and hiding rocks and pebbles in all sorts of public places to be found by others. Finders can either keep the rock or move them to somewhere else and share their finds on social media. Facebook pages are popping up as people set up groups in towns and cities to promote the craze. How could the RE teacher use this idea with the pupils do you think? It is one fad, but how do you remain aware of what is important in the pupils' lives in order to link with their interests? Do you watch children's television, read their latest books, visit toy shops or departments …? Or maybe you simply make time to ask them (Figure 4.12).

Look at some of the other images of the stones and pebbles. In RE you could design stones for the Buddhist five precepts, the three jewels of Buddhism, the ten commandments, the fruits of the spirit, the 5Ks of Sikhism or other sets of religious concepts.

Figure 4.11 Ebenezer, by McLean Bible Church in Washington, USA

Figure 4.12 Painted rocks (from http://www.thepilot.com/news/sp-church-stages-town-wide-scavenger-hunt-with-painted-rocks/article_a61aba3e-1bbf-11e7-b9d3-eb18560a3f17.html)

Trees are as richly symbolic as stones, and the next task asks you to investigate some tree symbolism.

Task seven: Trees

Use the concept of trees to work out some ideas for RE. You might think about

- artworks you can use,
- trees in literature,
- the Tree of Life,
- the tree of the knowledge of good and evil,
- *The Tale of Three Trees* by Angela Elwell Hunt and Tim Jonke (2001),
- The Jewish festival of Tu BiShvat,
- The Bodhi Tree of Bodh Gaya.

Look at how Louis has incorporated a tree into his ideas about The Golden Rule (Figure 4.13).

Figure 4.13 The Golden Rule, by Louis (aged 8)

My picture is showing The Golden Rule

I have drawn a tree because a tree to me stands up pointing to the sky and God is in the sky. The Golden Rule is at the top of the tree because it is so important to God and to ourselves. The tree is standing tall and firm like The Golden Rule helps us to stand up and live our lives doing the right thing. I wrote 'trust' up the sides of the tree because we have to trust ourselves to do the right thing. The red flower shows love. The Golden Rule is 'Treat other people how you want to be treated', so the people under the tree are holding hands to show care, friendship and support.

Getting arty

You have already encountered the *Spirited Arts* ideas earlier in this book and examples of art from this competition have been used throughout this book with permission. This section considers more about how art, design and RE can be good partners. However, occasionally when student teachers make links with other subjects, it is the RE component that becomes impoverished. This may be due to some of the insecurities about teaching the subject already unearthed in the first chapter. Despite this, cross-curricular links made wisely can enhance the subject greatly. Art is used as an exemplar here as often RE is grouped with the humanities but as Copley shows, 'epistemologically, RE has far more in common with the creative arts than with history and geography' (Copley 2005, p 115). The question becomes, 'why?'.

In medieval times, when only very few people outside the established church could read or write, art was used as a teaching source. Religious art has been used 'not only to edify and enlighten, but also to stir the emotions, instil faith, offer comfort, and inspire devotion' (de Rynck 2009, p 9). As both art and RE have the power to evoke awe and wonderment and raise questions about different meanings, the images call for skills of expression beyond the literal through symbol, metaphor and analogy (Cooling 2009). Blaylock (2004) confirms that RE, art and the expression of religious belief share certain characteristics. In art as in RE there are many ways to interpret something. Its use in RE helps learners gain new insights, prompts new questions and helps to address matters of complexity in understanding religion and belief. Woods, in writing about what art can bring to RE, notes 'works of art can express the verbally inexpressible [… and] great art can move people intellectually, emotionally and spiritually [… so] some people will engage visually with a work of art while others will engage emotionally with the people in the image' (http://www.rethinking.co.uk).

The following asks you to take a Hindu and Sikh celebration to demonstrate how art links can be forged for practical learning in RE. A carousel style of learning enables the pupils to engage with all the activities, spending a short time at each.

Raksha Bandhan (Figure 4.14) is celebrated in parts of India to celebrate family life, especially the relationship of siblings. There are various legends behind the festival relating to the various avatars (representations of Brahma) tying bands of protection and blessing on each other. Raksha Bandhan means 'bond of protection' and refers to the phenomenon of unconditional love given by brothers and sisters. The festival presents families with an opportunity to celebrate love and care. It is celebrated through gathering together as a family, praying, exchanging sweets and gifts, making Rangoli patterns and rakhi cards, singing and dancing and giving of rakhis. Rakhis are bracelets (made by younger sisters from various materials or from gold and other precious metals) given by sisters to their brothers. In return, brothers give gifts, promising to protect and stand by their sisters through times of good and hardship. On the day of festival, the ritual of giving the rakhi begins with a prayer. The sister then ties the rakhi around the brother's wrist and wishes him happiness and well-being. She puts roli and rice on her brother's forehead to show him blessing and gives him something sweet to eat. The day normally ends with a family meal where such foods as banana cutlets, vegetable pancakes and tamarind rice are enjoyed.

Search on YouTube to witness the celebration (Figure 4.15).

Figure 4.14 Raksha Bandhan (from http://www.raksha-bandhan.com/rakhi-the-thread-of-love.html)

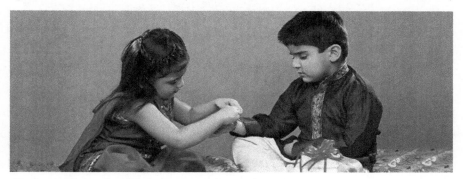

Task eight: Raksha Bandhan

Using a carousel for Raksha Bandhan. Taking the detail from http://www.raksha-bandhan.com/rakhi-the-thread-of-love.html, plan a lesson for reception-aged pupils. Discover art and design links without losing the RE and design a carousel of activities. It is probably best to spend a half day on this teaching and learning. Invite parents into school to help.

Present the material in a way that makes sense to young pupils and ensure that bridges are built with their own experience. Consider how you will draw all the learning together through a plenary that reinforces the explicit material from the religion.

Ami, aged 7, includes the words 'love', 'protect' and 'caring' in her picture. For her, these are the concepts that emerge clearly from studying the festival.

Figure 4.15 Love, Protect, Caring, by Ami

There is a Hindu festival for brothers and sisters called Raksha Bandhan. In our story a little girl made a bracelet for her brother. In return she made him promise to look after her. He then gave her some money. In my picture they love each other and are being nice to each other. The hearts show how brothers and sisters love each other.

Art in Islam is a particularly good theme to explore with pupils. A focus on Tawhid (the Oneness of God) can be used and pupils can learn how this concept is represented in all of life including Islamic art. Religion encompasses the aesthetic in Islam, as evidenced in the architecture of the Alhambra in Spain. Remember that some Muslim pupils will not be allowed to draw people or animals in their art. (Do you know why?) Islamic art usually focuses on pattern, order and nature and these disciplines are also seen in the rituals of Islamic practice such as prayer, fasting and feasting, pilgrimage and attending the mosque. Good links can be made with tessellated patterns in maths. Using a 10-by-10-centimetre-squared paper grid with the axes drawn, pupils can copy and (better still) create their own designs, and the 10-by-10 pattern can be traced and replicated on a bigger piece of paper. As the shape is joined to the next one, new shapes and forms will be created. The pupils can use colour symbolism including black and white, the use of green for the colour of paradise, blue for infinity and revelation, yellow for glory and plenty. This will help the pupils understand the symbolism of patterns and of colours. To make this an RE lesson you will need to explain to the pupils the links between belief, practice and worship. Look at and practice calligraphy with the pupils too.

There are many links to art that can be used in a study of Hindu and Muslim practice, as in the examples above. In general terms, art provides an extraordinarily rich resource for RE. Pupils can study paintings, sculpture, statues, fabrics, collage, architecture, calligraphy and stained glass windows used in worship. Through bringing their understanding to a religious image, the pupil accomplishes a creative act, and dialogue can be started and sustained. There are various excellent resources that have been designed to help pupils engage with art and RE, motivating pupils to create their own works of art in response. Look at those created by the following publishers (there are more):

- The Stapleford Centre (http://www.stapleford-centre.org/).
- RE Today Publications (http://www.retoday.org.uk/publications).
- Religious and Moral Educational Press (RMEP) (https://rmep.hymnsam.co.uk/).

Summary

This chapter has considered just a few ways to make RE a practical and dynamic subject. We have not included making foodstuff or drama or many other forms but you can experiment. With an imaginative teacher, willing to take risks and understand what attracts pupils at the time, the opportunities to use practical methods and to link with the pupils' lives are endless. Perhaps you might try some of the activities introduced in this chapter with your pupils. Remember that it is important that you retain the explicit RE throughout the activity so that the pupils develop knowledge and understanding of religion and worldviews. You will need to talk about why you are doing what you are doing. Practical RE can be full of surprise, something we both feel is an important aspect of RE and of all learning.

Recommended reading

Cooling, M (2009) *Christianity through Art: A Resource for Teaching Religious Education through Art*; Norwich: RMEP.
Lewis, C S (2000) *The Complete Chronicles of Narnia*; London: HarperCollins.

Chapter 5
Skills to Develop in Religious Education

Chapter objectives

- What is enquiry learning in RE?
- Why is enquiry learning in RE important?
- Tackling an ultimate enquiry: God
- What skills can be developed in effective enquiry learning in RE?
- Relational RE
- How can using enquiry skills develop pupils' autonomy and agency?

Introduction

In this chapter, we consider the place of enquiry-based learning in RE. Enquiry learning is sometimes called problem- or brain-based learning and is active and experiential, not passive. The themes of this chapter therefore build on those presented in Chapter 4. Linking enquiry forms of learning to the higher thinking skills presented in Bloom's taxonomy (Bloom 1965, Bloom et al. 1965) may be useful for you in understanding what Bloom's skills are and how they may develop through effective RE. You will consider how RE can help pupils develop as critical thinkers as they learn to consider the claims made by religions and worldviews and so develop a greater sense of agency and autonomy.

What is enquiry learning in RE?

Enquiry learning in RE that is both active and affective can progress the development of the pupils' cognitive and meta-cognitive (the way they think about their thinking) domains. However, it can do more than that. As Gates says

> RE does indeed have an interest in promoting cognitive development. It has vehicles and resources that lend themselves to stretching of thought and imagination.

It is not at all shy of wanting to engage pupils in wondering why this, and that, and the other. A curriculum that invites them to wonder cannot help but be about development.

(Gates, in Broadbent and Brown 2002, p 108)

Enquiry-based study in RE, as in other subjects, involves the three learning fields of knowledge, skills and attitudes that Bloom considers to be the goals of learning and that you have already explored in this text – with the addition of 'concepts' – through using CASK. It concerns learner-led and not teacher-centred pedagogy. Watson and Thompson believe it is essential to develop thinking skills in RE, and this will help the subject to be taken more seriously, academically and intellectually. There is an assumption here that it is not considered this way by some. Is this your experience? They argue that RE must develop the pupils' thinking skills as without these, pupils cannot 'evaluate for themselves the truth of religious belief'.

Without the development of such reflective, critical thinking skills, children have no means of resisting cultural pressures such as relativism or fully developing their religious understanding.

(Watson and Thompson 2006, p 29)

Mastery of RE can be developed through brain-based learning that encourages independence and autonomy of thought, so perhaps a pupil might identify their quality of learning through some of the following statements. You might like to rewrite them so that they are more age appropriate or child-friendly or you might think they are fine as they are for the pupils you teach.

I show mastery in RE when I

- link prior to current learning in logical ways,
- apply my knowledge and understanding in new contexts,
- generate questions to extend my learning and know how to answer these through my own investigations,
- model my learning to others and provide clear explanations,
- teach other pupils and adults to understand, more deeply, the religious concepts being studied,
- present findings clearly and coherently in practical, written, multimedia formats – whichever are most suitable,
- draw links and relationships between different ideas,
- retain my curiosity to find out new things.

Helping pupils to remain curious will call on you to find ways to arouse interest and motivation to discover for themselves. The following activity draws on the pupils' ability to learn from resources, use their senses and link ideas.

These slides are taken from a colleague's resources used in teaching about the Jewish festival of Pesach (Passover). To begin their learning, pupils need to research the account of Passover (Pesach) in the Old Testament/Torah, found in Exodus Chapters 5–14. They will also need to discover what a Seder plate is and how it is associated with the narrative. As you consider the following ideas for pupils' learning, you may have to research these aspects for yourself (Figures 5.1–5.5).

Figure 5.1 Pesach plate

Figure 5.2 Taste and smell

SENSORY CAROUSEL

Figure 5.3 Look

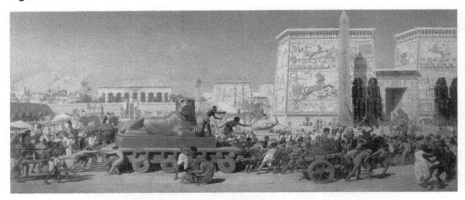

SENSORY CAROUSEL

Figure 5.4 Listen

Chorus Of The Hebrew Slaves

Fly, thought, on wings of gold,
go settle upon the slopes and the hills
where the sweet airs of our
native soil smell soft and mild!
Greet the banks of the river Jordan
and Zion's tumbled towers.
Oh, my country, so lovely and lost!
Oh remembrance so dear yet unhappy!

Golden harp of the prophetic wise men,
why hang so silently from the willows?
Rekindle the memories in our hearts,
tell us about the times gone by!
Remembering the fate of Jerusalem
play us a sad lament
or else be inspired by the Lord
to fortify us to endure our suffering!

SENSORY CAROUSEL

Figure 5.5 Feel

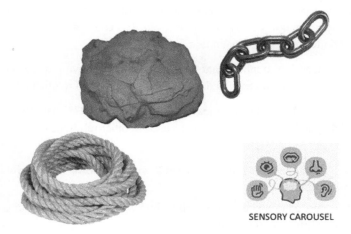

SENSORY CAROUSEL

Mary, the teacher-trainer who taught this session, focused the pupils' learning on what slavery must have felt like for the Jewish people and what it means to be free. She describes her sensory, enquiry-based lesson ideas for pupils in the following:

The idea is to encourage deeper thinking and questioning about the Jewish festival of Pesach. The focus for this is the Seder meal, discussed using the Seder plate. The children must discover the account for themselves using the resources and their senses. There are three main activities.

- Activity 1: Use of the Seder plate as the basis for discussion of the story from Exodus retold at the Seder meal by some Jewish families at Pesach.

- Activity 2: The children examine the account in the Old Testament/Torah, using a child-appropriate version of the text.

- Activity 3: Development of learning: carousel to gain a sense of what slavery means and why it is important for Jewish people to celebrate their freedom from slavery. Each table is visited in turn. After each sensory experience the child writes one or two words on a strip of coloured paper to describe their thought/emotions/feelings about slavery.

The sensory carousel tables:

- Table 1: Taste and smell: bitter herbs dipped in salt water, grated horseradish, matzos.

- Table 2: Look: magnifying glasses to look at details of pictures of slavery in Egyptian times.

- Table 3: Listen: Verdi's Chorus of the Hebrew Slaves from Nabucco (which has identifiable and interesting contrasts from sadness and suffering to hope and joy).

- Table 4: Feel: bricks, chain, rope.

At the end we link all the strips with words describing slavery together to form a long paper chain. Children could develop this further by composing their own slavery song/poem using the words in the chain. This could also include dance/music composition to show the different emotions.

Following this learning, pupils might also explore the following questions through individual or group investigation and feedback what they find to others:

- Why do Jewish people use unleavened bread at Pesach? What other types of bread do you know? Are any of these used in other religious traditions?
- What is the Haggadah?
- Who initiates the telling of the story at Pesach and how? Why do you think this is important?
- What is needed to make charoset and why? What other food would you include to bring out the meaning of the story?
- What do the other foods represent on the Seder plate?
- What other special meals do Jewish children share with others and why? What might the children do at these meals?
- What special meals do you celebrate and why? What traditions do you have at these times? What do you remember?

You can begin the process of enquiry-based learning with pupils through posing open-ended questions, problems, issues and scenarios. Rather than presenting established facts that need no further investigation, knowledge in this case is not portrayed as smooth and merely to be accepted. Rather, knowledge is seen as problematic and troublesome, and often, in the case of religions and non-religious worldviews, highly contested. Facilitating enquiry-based learning enables pupils to find out for themselves through gathering and analysing data, then reprocessing (rather than regurgitating) information and so taking it apart and reorganizing it.

In such learning, pupils do not expect to be harassed to provide quick answers without time to think. Look at Alan Ahlberg's poem *The Question* in his collection *I Heard it in the Playground* (Ahlberg 1991) and stand a while in the shoes of the poor child and feel as the child felt. Deep learning can often call for space and is demanding of an opportunity to 'dwell' in and on the material.

Problem-based learning is aligned with constructivist theories and philosophies of learning and so draws on the thinking of such theorists as Dewey, Vygotsky and Bandura. Dewey was keen on children developing critical thinking skills and investigation methods. It is worth spending a little more time discussing these forms of learning. Bandura and Vygotsky support socially constructive classrooms where collaborative investigations happen through developing questions, clarifying through discussion, predicting and summarizing. In such methods of teaching and learning, new knowledge is built on existing knowledge and so is effectively scaffolded. 'Constructivists … tend to look at each pupil's current understanding or "worldview" (whatever subject is being studied), and see teaching and learning as building on, or reconstructing, that worldview' (Stern 2018a, p 63). Pupils can generate information and reconstruct meaning in social situations, so that much of the learning is grounded in group work that diminishes the competitive and combative nature of some educational strategy.

Others write about constructivist ways of learning. You may find the following helpful for your understanding. Of course, such thinking needs to be put to work and it is up to you, the teacher, to translate the theory into classroom practice:

> Constructivism is a philosophical approach according to which all knowledge is 'constructed' in as much as it is reliant upon convention, human perception and social experience. ... Learning takes place when pupils revisit current knowledge and adjust, adapt or revise it in order to incorporate new ideas.
>
> (Erricker et al. 2011, p 37)

We particularly like what Freire adds when he states 'knowledge emerges only through invention and reinvention; through restless, impatient, confusing, hopeful inquiry, human beings pursue in the world, with the world and each other' (Freire 1993, p 53). This seems particularly fitting for the subject of RE.

Such learning needs to take place in an atmosphere conducive to cooperative study where pupils can become active researchers. How might you organize your classroom so that it is suited to such study? Some appropriate tasks involved in enquiry-based learning might include role-play and debate and online discussion that asks pupils to explore various perspectives while learning to show respect for individual viewpoints. Other activities might include case studies, simulations, games and learning cells where pairs of pupils research, devise questions about their subject matter and then are paired with another two to begin discussion and further research.

To record their discussion, pupils might compile a mind map of their thinking as a group, writing their ideas on a paper tablecloth and then moving round in groups adding further ideas to the cloths presented by others.

Here is an example of how a teaching colleague, Claire, uses enquiry-based learning with pupils. The story used is found in the Christian Bible Luke Chapter 5, Verses 17–26, and is an account of a paralysed man being lowered through the ceiling to see Jesus (Figure 5.6).

The pupils enter the classroom to see a model of a flat-roofed house in the style used in Jesus's time. The house has a hole in the roof with debris that has fallen to the floor inside. On the floor, there is what looks like a stretcher and discarded blanket. The house has police tape round the outside and the pupils assume the role of detectives, examining the evidence, asking questions and offering hypotheses of what has happened. They wonder how else they might find out about the incident and talk about eye witness accounts. Some pupils from another class might act as eye witnesses later in the investigation. (You might put a paper shape of a hole in the ceiling of the classroom and spread dust and debris below and add the bed and blanket, while cordoning off the room with police tape.)

Once they have talked and hypothesized, the pupils can turn to the Biblical account and read for themselves, puzzling out what has happened and asking new questions

Figure 5.6 Take up your mat and walk (from https://pilgrimjustpilgrim.wordpress.com/)

to further the enquiry. In this, they look at a primary source and can ask what Christians believe about this account and what it portrays about the person of Jesus for them. So, in this activity, the pupils need to form a hypothesis, find evidence that supports their answers to a question, collect and consider information as they revisit their hypothesis and then re-evaluate the data. They also need to enter a different culture to understand the context of the account. As Copley shows, 'removed from the originating culture and presented without any clues to that culture, religious stories can be seriously misunderstood' (Copley 2005, p 124). This will require research.

Task one: Setting up a learning scene

Choose a headline from the following or make up one from another account found in religious literature and think about how you might set up a learning scene for the pupils to investigate. Decide what props and clues you would provide:

- Boy develops elephant's head (Ganesh, Shiva and Parvati).
- Twelve baskets of food found on hillside (the feeding of the 5,000).
- Blood discovered on multicoloured coat (Joseph and his jealous brothers).
- Missing body – burial cloths folded in tomb (Jesus's resurrection).

Why is enquiry learning in RE important?

Enquiry learning often begins with questions. In RE, where some of the ultimate questions become the focus, this is good news. Pupils live in a world of questions, daily, but are rarely asked to voice their own questions. You will be able to facilitate space where this becomes possible, but be aware that these questions may cause deviation from the best planned lesson. You might ask the pupils to log the questions that they have encountered or considered in the last twenty-four hours and categorize them according to their kind. They should note whether the questions are trivial, important, can be simply answered and whether this is important. Pupils might be asked how types of questions that have no simple solutions make them feel. Some student teachers are afraid of developing a pedagogy of question, in case they encounter conflict or do not know answers. They often write about helping pupils feel comfortable in RE lessons, but soon come to see there is much that can become challenging for both teacher and pupil alike, especially as pupils bring in assumptions and prejudices from their homes and prevailing cultures. Ultimate questions will always challenge and as Copley says, 'education does not always have to be about making people cosy; it can exercise a prophetic function as well, in other words it can call people to reconsider their entrenched attitudes and values or see how their culture might have programmed them into certain modes of thought' (Copley 2005, p 87).

Gates maintains that ultimate questions and theological and philosophical pondering should be central to effective RE. He maintains that RE promotes thinking skills at all ages and 'at the same time gives companionship to boys and girls in facing any tussles, which they find themselves in, regarding overall purpose and meaning in life and death' (Gates, in Broadbent and Brown 2002, p 108). Mason maintains that at its best 'RE is an open-minded and inclusive search for answers to the kinds of questions that all human beings, whatever their beliefs and traditions, ask about life and death and about values, purpose and meaning'. She adds that 'humanist perspectives are relevant to that "personal search"' (https://humanism.org.uk/). It is part of being a curious human being to ask questions. An example of an ultimate question could be 'Why am I here?' The pupils can discover how different religions and worldviews answer this as well as articulating their own ideas.

Task two: Ultimate questions

- Devise a list of ultimate questions that might become the focus of RE.
- Choose one and think about how you might use this as the focus in RE.
- Consider the challenges and the opportunities this might raise for the pupils.
- How much do you already know about what others from a religious or non-religious perspective might offer as an answer to your chosen question?
- How might you find out?
- How do you answer this ultimate question at present?

This last question is important if you agree with Teece's comment that RE teachers must bring the same openness and exploration to the subject that they expect from the pupils and need to care about processes of learning too. He says that we need to 'increase our understanding of the place of religion in people's lives by relating what we learn about the religions to our own deepest questions of meaning and purpose' (Teece 2001, p 66).

Perhaps with Leah aged eleven, people might ask the following:

> If God is with us, why is the world full of pain?
>
> God made us a perfect world, a good world, supposedly. I don't understand how God can be such a good person if he created a world with pain. In my picture there is a girl searching or the world God created. The one that is good, full of morality and peace. She doesn't believe that the world she knows is the world God created. Neither do I, but it makes me question. Does God understand that to recognise the good, you need bad things to happen? Like light needs dark to exist. Like in my picture there are two sides to it. One all black and full of pain and nothingness, the other peaceful and happy. (Figure 5.7)

Or with Daisy, aged six, they might enquire, 'Why do we have colour?'.

> Imagine the world without colour, everything would be grey and dull. I have painted my background light grey so that when the box of colour is opened it gives people a surprise with all the bright beautiful colours. I think God had a special power to make colour and I think we should help God by looking after our wonderful colourful world. I like the materials I have used because they are like all the things we have on Earth and it is like the song we sing in assembly (Who put colours in the rainbow). (Figure 5.8)

Figure 5.7 Why is the world full of pain?, by Leah (aged eleven)

Figure 5.8 Why do we have colour?, by Daisy (aged six)

Seaman and Owen suggest that teachers will always feel a sense of inadequacy in dealing with life's ultimate questions in the classroom but urge them to take the opportunity in thinking about the ultimate questions for themselves as they teach pupils. 'We are all in our own way grappling with mystery', they say, 'and by giving the children the opportunity to explore their ideas, we are helping them to develop the skills, the language and the confidence to join us in that quest' (Seaman and Owen 2012, pp 2–3). Through considering ultimate questions, pupils can come to appreciate that there are issues concerned with the meaning of life and that there are mysteries to which we cannot always find an answer that satisfies. This should not prevent such questions from being asked, and pupils need to learn to live with uncertainty and ambiguity.

Watson and Thompson (2006) believe that at the heart of all religion lies mystery. However, people often want clear and pat answers. Why do you think this is so? These two authors argue for the need for imagination as a means of understanding more of reality, and stress the need for humility, too, when it comes to considering religion. Copley says that we often ask the wrong questions that close exploration down. He says that when dealing with the ultimate questions of life, the teacher should promote a 'greater humility of inquiry' (Copley 2005, p 19) than is sometimes the case. Why do you think all writers mention the need for humility and why is this virtue particularly important for the RE teacher? Watson and Thompson maintain the following:

All the great religions affirm that at the heart of religion lies Mystery which nothing can adequately express: all religious forms of expression have the character of pointing towards this mystery and not describing it. … In religion 'mystery' does not indicate a problem to be solved. The kind of response which it calls forth is not a factual wonder why but a wonder at. It does not question as such but accepts the givenness of mystery which arouses awe and even adoration. … For awareness of Mystery brings a paradox: at the same time religious people claim to have knowledge of this Mystery they become more deeply aware that it is infinitely beyond any understanding.

(Watson and Thompson 2006, p 114)

Tackling an ultimate enquiry: God

In most religions, God is seen to be at the heart of mystery if not the mystery itself, but many student teachers feel unprepared to teach a series of lessons exploring God. Some say, 'I do not believe in God so that would be difficult for me', and others, 'this is a huge subject and I would not know where to start, what question would I begin with'. It is our opinion that pupils take great delight in discussing existential and theological matters especially when their views are taken seriously. As you have seen in previous chapters, pupils can grapple with huge questions providing they are considered in age-appropriate ways. For example, pupils can begin to understand the Trimurti and avatars of Hinduism when they consider who they, themselves, are and appear to different people – learner, brother/sister, daughter/son, friend, helper and so on. They can understand why Hindu children pray to Ganesh when they start a new school when they know this avatar is called the Remover of Obstacles. They can appreciate the Trimurti as they link this with the need for the circle of life. (Can we hear Elton John singing?)

Pupils have wonderful things to say about God. The following comments are taken from RE Festival responses, research conducted in 1997. Why not use the question that elicited these replies with pupils you teach and then use their writing with other pupils as a stimulus for their own thinking to emerge.

Question: Some people feel that God can help you, or cheer you up, or warn you, or that God is watching you. Have you ever felt someone or something near you in this kind of way? Write about how you felt.

I don't believe in God (seven-year-old)

I felt like God was watching me and trying to say something (seven-year-old)

my grandad died I felt as if part of me was broken and god was fixing it (seven-year-old)

Dear Friend, when I have problems or get told off by my teacher I always go home and tell god. That always makes me feel better. It made me feel a bit like an angel touched me with her golden finger. It was like a dream. Mostly I felt like that when I was lonely (eight-year-old)

Leah, aged ten, wrote the following:

> I think of God as my family when I need love, my friend when I am lonely and my teacher when I'm naughty. I think of him as a kind, loving, gentle and a very important person in my life.

Leah makes sense of God in terms of what she recognizes of others. This is not surprising in the face of trying to explain the indescribable. Rudolph Otto writing in 1923 maintained the following:

> All language, in so far as it consists of words, purports to convey ideas or concepts – that is what language means – and the more clearly and unequivocally it does so the better the language. And hence expositions of religious truth in language inevitably tend to stress the 'rational' attributes of God.
>
> (Otto 1958, p 2)

It is no wonder then that scriptures speak about God in terms of metaphor or why art is such a strong ally to teaching RE effectively. Ewens and Stone (2001, p 21) include some pupils' metaphors for God. They asked the seven- and eight-year-old pupils to consider: 'If God were a _____ what would God be?'. The pupils responded as follows:

- God is like a dove because he likes peace.
- If God were a flower he'd be a sunflower because he brings light to the world.
- If God were a flower he would be a rose near my grandma's grave.
- He's like a jeep. He can go anywhere.

Taken from the Spirited Poetry of 2011, Alice Brewer, aged eleven, writes the following:

> *Where God Is!*
> God is in the whirring of the world spinning round,
> God is the day before the first king was crowned.
> God is the beauty of an ever changing sky,
> God is the changing of the moon's phases going by.
> God is the feel of rough bark from a tree,
> At the same time a supernova exploding miles away from me.
> God is the smell of a frosty morning,
> God is a mother calling her children – nervous and warning.
> God isn't a person, he is nature and science for me,
> But most of all I think God is free.

Copley shows the limitations of such a question as, 'Do you believe in God?' He points out that the only God worth talking about is one that cannot be talked about in such terms. God becomes a proposition, while the important questions about how religious people make sense of their being through faith in God remain unexplored or developed. He writes that

> education should embrace the possibility of God. That is not the same as embracing the certainty of God, in the face of which one could only instruct students to believe, or to try to compel faith – in other words indoctrinate. … The central question should not be whether we 'believe in' God but rather, 'what does it mean to take God seriously?'
>
> (Copley 2005, p 139)

As Hull (1991) emphasized, it is not the teacher's role to pass on any correct or ortho-dox doctrine of God. That is the remit of faith communities. Instead, the teacher's task is to enlarge the pupils' vocabulary and religious literacy so that they might be able to grapple with issues and experiences and develop images and concepts that will help them enter the conversation that constitutes what he saw as 'God-talk'. 'Good RE teaching must not ignore the theological and God-centred dimensions of Bible narratives' (Stern 2018a, p 91).

Task three: God talk

- In the light of what these writers say, how would you begin to teach about what different religious and non-religious people say about God?

Perhaps the following questions might help as you think about the different religions and non-religious worldviews that you might teach about in the primary sector. What is the name of God or deity? How does God make Godself known? (For example, through prophets, messengers, life experiences, through the Holy Spirit and Son, scriptures.) How do people worship God? What does God demand from followers? (For example, through obedience, trust, worship, service.) Why do some people not acknowledge a God?

- Use the ideas presented in this chapter with pupils.
- Ask the pupils for metaphors: see if any of their metaphors match with the ones in religious writings.
- Let the pupils respond in word association, if God was a colour, sound, animal, person, place, bird, flower. Then let the pupils compare their answers and use these as a basis for discussion. Talk with them about the variety of answers and what that might show.
- Ask the pupils to draw something of God, if there were a God. (You may well be surprised by their responses, and all pupils can join in as you are not asking pupils to draw God, and you are not assuming they are positive about God's existence.)
- Use the themes used by Spirited Arts (https://www.natre.org.uk/about-na-tre/projects/spirited-arts/) and look at other pupils' artistic responses before reading what they write about their images

Arthur, who is six years old, sums up his understanding here, very succinctly (Figure 5.9):

God in Time

God is in time and is very adventurous.

Figure 5.9 God in time, by Arthur (aged six)

Emma tells what she thinks God does (Figure 5.10):

I drew this picture because it really expresses my feelings about God in a way meaning I'm the boat and the sea is my life. It is stormy because I'm making a bad choice and going to the rocks but God is in the lighthouse and warning me of danger. For me, the rocks represent my temptations and bad choices, but sometimes I ignore the warning and I crash into the rocks and face the consequences for what I have done but because Jesus died on the cross I'm forgiven my sins and I can sail again!

Figure 5.10 Lighthouse, by Emma (aged ten)

Would you be surprised if a child showed such personal conviction by saying these things? What would you say to Emma? How would you continue the lesson and involve other pupils to include all?

Emma sees God as both her Guide and Saviour. Here are a few ideas concerning Islamic belief about God, using the names of God, and accompanied by a number of associated areas to explore in italics:

- Muslims maintain in the Shahadah 'I bear witness that there is no God but Allah, (the One) and Muhammad is the prophet of Allah'. *How is this like a creed and who else uses creeds?*

- A Muslim's ninety-nine beautiful names of Allah include some offering comfort such as the Source of Peace, the Bestower, the All-Seeing, the Protecting Friend, the Pardoner. Others emphasize different aspects such as the Avenger, Presenter, Reckoner, All-Forgiving, Most Merciful, Most Great, Just, Source of Goodness, All-Seeing, Guide, Wise, Truth, Most Generous, Creator, Protector, Light, Compassionate. *Select two of the names and explain what they show of Allah and Allah's dealings with people.*

- Human beings recite these names often using *tasbih*, prayer beads, sets of thirty-three or ninety-nine beads. Why 99 and not 100 beads? *What titles would the pupils give to someone they know very well and why? Could they make a necklace where these titles are celebrated/remembered?*

- Muslims are taught to begin each day 'In the name of God, the Merciful, the Compassionate'. These words are found at the beginning of every chapter in the Qur'an except one. *Why is it important for a believer to repeat their beliefs frequently? What difference would it make if they stopped doing this?* (Figure 5.11).

You might do the following:

- Begin by asking the pupils to spend time talking about how beads and ornaments are used in religions, such as WWJD bracelets and the Sikh kara.

Figure 5.11 Prayer beads

- Ask about the times they would want special beads to remember – a happy, sad, difficult time? A special person?
- Choose a bead for each memory, choosing the colour very carefully and thread them on elastic. How might you develop this idea further?

Task four: Hindu ideas of God

Here are four slides that we use with student teachers as we consider teaching about Hinduism. The first idea is taken from Ewens and Stone (2001).

- Consider how you might use these with pupils to teach about aspects of God. You will have to access an image of Ganesh that you can show to the pupils. How will you teach in a way that elicits pupils' ideas rather than simply introducing the slides and 'going through' them? (Figures 5.12–5.14).

Figure 5.12 Visually create a character

- Lord of Time
- Message Giver
- Lord of Power
- Problem Solver
- Lady of Learning
- Lord of all Weather
- Lady of Peace

Figure 5.13 Ganesh

The remover of all obstacles
the god of new beginnings

- The son of Parvarti and Shiva
- Four arms and a broken tusk
- He may carry sweets, a water lily or a conch shell
- He rides around on a rat
- He wears a sacred thread

- In some parts of India there is a festival dedicated to him
- He may carry a hatchet
- He has prayer beads
- His mudra says 'do not fear'
- There is a cobra round his waist

Figure 5.14 Hindu creation story

Before the world was created, there was nothing but water.

Out of the murky dark waters, a single lotus flower had begun to grow with Brahma the creator sitting on it.

The Lord Vishnu spoke to Brahma and told him it was the time for the world to be created.

Brahma divided the lotus in three parts. The first became heaven, the second became the earth
and the third was the sky.

A faint sound grew louder …aum aum aum until everywhere was filled with it.

Suddenly the world was full of newly created creatures.

Brahma divided his body into two parts and from one part he made man and from the other he made woman

Pause for thought

A Year 1 class designed a Hindu 'shrine' in their classroom. The teacher made it very clear that the pupils were not to offer prayers or offerings at this shrine. Pupils painted Hindu deities and learned about how some Hindus pray to Ganesh when starting something new. They added paper flowers and decorated with tinsel, paper chains, decorations and a candle and talked about why. The teacher added a puja tray to the shrine consisting of a tray, bell, diva lamp, kum kum powder, spoon water pot and introduced the word *Arti*. She read the words 'I accept that gift devotedly given from the giver who gives himself' from the Hindu text (Bhagavad Gita, 9.26), and they watched the Water part of a DVD called Water, Moon, Candle, Tree and Sword produced by Channel 4. An invited Hindu teacher talked about the shrine at her mandir and the one she had at home. The pupils went on to make individual Hindu shrines in a shoebox and labelled the contents. They enjoyed the activity and seemed to learn so much that the teacher thought the session might be repeated for a Buddhist shrine or Christian altar with a set of 'stained glass' images for the background.

What do you think about this activity? Is it one that you would do with your pupils? Why or why not?

What skills can be developed in effective enquiry learning in RE?

There are many skills and attitudes developed in effective enquiry learning in RE and the following links these with what Bloom developed as his taxonomy (Figure 5.15).

This graphic, released under a Creative Commons attribution license, provides a quick overview of Bloom's taxonomy of the kinds of cognitive processes often asked of students in educational settings. The graphic reflects the 2001 revision of

Figure 5.15 Bloom's taxonomy

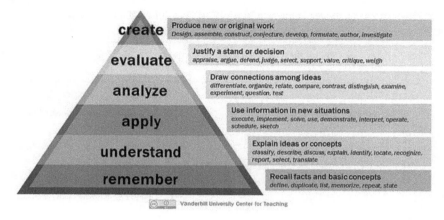

the original Bloom's taxonomy of educational objectives, with the top two categories swapped around. (For more on Bloom's taxonomy, see the Vanderbilt University Center for Teaching guide on the subject: https://cft.vanderbilt.edu/guides-sub-pages/blooms-taxonomy/)

Making use of Bloom's original taxonomy of skills, mostly identified under the areas of knowledge, comprehension, application, analysis, synthesis and evaluation, can help the teacher to plan teaching and learning that takes the pupils beyond the stage of regurgitating to reprocessing and applying subject knowledge. This taxonomy is often presented as a hierarchy, but could be presented as circular as teachers learn to develop divergent thinkers as well as deep rather than surface learning.

The following provides an extensive list of verbs, question starters, potential activities and assessment opportunities. You may find the information in the grid useful in constructing learning objectives and teaching strategies in RE. As your own knowledge and understanding of the subject material in RE develops, add detail to the grid.

Task five: Blooming RE

Add four possible activities or assessment opportunities to the grid below.

Verbs	Some key words and question starters	Possible activities or assessment opportunities
Knowledge (remember)	Recall facts and basic concepts	
Define Describe Find	Who, what, why, when, where, which. How would you describe …?	Recount the Sikh story of Diwali. Describe how a Muslim prays. Find places of worship in the locale.

Verbs	Some key words and question starters	Possible activities or assessment opportunities
Knowledge (remember)	**Recall facts and basic concepts**	
Identify Name, list, label Match Memorize Recall, recount Recognize, relate Select Write	How would you explain ...? Can you recall ...? Who was it that ...? Can you name the ...? Describe what happened at ...? Can you tell why ...? Find the meaning of ...? Which is true or false ...?	List the ten plagues in order. Label the days of creation according to the Biblical narrative. Recognize and list ways we belong. Recall a timeline of the Christmas events. Make a facts chart about a place of worship. Select the golden rules for the classroom. Write an acrostic poem about yourself using your name as the guide. Memorize and recite a poem/song/verse that is important for a Buddhist.
Comprehension (understand)	**Demonstrate understanding of facts and ideas**	
Compare Contrast Classify Describe Discuss Distinguish Explain Illustrate Interpret Outline Predict Relate Rephrase Restate Summarize Translate	How would you compare ...? Rephrase the following ... Which ideas or facts show ...? How would you summarize ...? Write a brief outline of ...? What might happen next ...? Who do you think ...? What was the main idea ...? Who was the key character ...? Can you distinguish between ...? Can you provide an example of what you mean ...? Provide a definition for ...? What is meant by ...?	What do you think this artist is saying ...? Draw the next scene of this event/ritual ... Predict what will happen to the characters in ... Summarize how the people felt at the start, the middle and the end of the account of ... Illustrate what you think the main idea in ... was through drama. Write and perform a play based on the story of ... Paint a picture of some aspect you don't understand about ... Prepare a flow chart to illustrate the sequence of events of ...

Application (apply)	**Use information in new situations by applying acquired knowledge**	
Apply Classify Complete Construct Demonstrate Develop Examine Experiment Identify Illustrate Interpret Model Organize Select Show Solve Use	How would you solve …? How would you apply what you have learned to develop …? What approach would you use …? Can you use these ideas to …? Do you know another instance where …? Can you group by characteristics such as …? What factors would you change if …? Can you apply the idea to your own experience …? What questions would you ask …? From the information given, can you develop a set of instructions about …?	You invite a Jew, Muslim and Hindu to a dinner party – what will you cook and why? If you decided to … what do you think would happen? Construct a model to demonstrate how a space will be used for teaching and worship. Make a diorama to illustrate an important event for … Take a collection of photographs to demonstrate your point about … Make up a puzzle game about what we have been learning. Design a marketing strategy for your new product to help … Write a textbook about … for others in a different class.
Analysis (analyse)	**Examine and break information into parts by making inferences and finding evidence to support reasons. Draw connections between ideas**	
Advertise Analyse Assume Categorize Compare Conclude Connect Contrast Distinguish	What conclusions can you draw …? How would you categorize …? What is the relationship between …? Why do you come to that assumption? What ideas justify …? What do you see as other possible outcomes?	Select parts of the account that are the hardest, saddest, most bewildering … Distinguish between fact/fiction/opinion/belief. What can you infer from the way that character behaved? What are the ideas behind the seven 'I Am' sayings of Jesus? Design a questionnaire to gather information.

Verbs	Some key words and question starters	Possible activities or assessment opportunities
Analysis (analyse)	**Examine and break information into parts by making inferences and finding evidence to support reasons. Draw connections between ideas**	
Examine Explain Identify Infer Investigate Organize Problematize Relate Separate Question	Can you explain what must have happened when …? How is … similar to …? What are some of the problems of …? Can you distinguish between …? What were some of the motives behind …? What was the turning point in the story/event? What was the problem with …?	Investigate to produce information to support a view. Make a flow chart to show the critical stages. Make a family tree showing relationships. Put on a play about … Write a biography of … Prepare a report about … Arrange a party for Hanukkah. Make all the arrangements and record the steps needed.
Synthesis (create)	**Compile information together in a different way by combining ideas/parts in a new pattern**	
Argue Change, compile Compose Construct Create Design Devise Evaluate Formulate Imagine Improve Invent Justify	How would you improve …? How could you change …? Suppose you could …? What do you think would happen if …? Can you think of an original way to …? Which ideas justify …? What evidence can you find for …? What is the relationship between …?	Write three new titles for a story, for example. 'the forgiving father' rather than 'the prodigal son' Write a different ending for … and note the implications of this Construct a poster about … that would … Compose a dialogue between … Write a song for … to perform about … Design a building to help Buddhists meditate … Create a new product. Give it a name and plan a marketing campaign for the community.

Plan	Can you design a … to …?	Design a book, magazine cover, … for …
Predict	Why don't you devise your own way to deal with …?	Devise a way to … following the rules for a …
Propose		
Solve	How many ways can you …?	
Test		Compose a rhythm or put new words to a known melody about …
Theorize		

Evaluation (evaluate)	**Present and defend opinions, validity of ideas. Produce new work and understand worth**	

Argue	What is your opinion of …?	Which character would you like to meet for a day and why?
Assess		
Choose	Would it be better if …?	Discuss whether the event could have happened and why you think that.
Conclude	What would you select to …?	
Construct		
Critique	What choice would you have made and why?	Conduct a debate about an issue of special interest for …
Debate		
Decide	Why was it better that …?	Make a booklet about five rules you see as important. Convince others they are the best.
	How would you judge …?	
Deduct	What information did you use to make your conclusion about …?	
Defend		Form a panel to discuss views about …
Design		
Discuss	Is there a better solution to …?	Write a letter to … advising on changes needed at …
Estimate		
Evaluate	Judge the value of …	Prepare a case to present your view about …
Interpret	Can you defend your position about …?	
Judge		
Justify	Do you think … is a good or a bad thing?	
Prioritize		
Rate	How would you have handled …?	
Recommend		
Select	What changes to … would you recommend?	
Verify	How would you feel if …?	
	How effective are …?	

Some of the ideas used in this grid are taken from Dalton and Smith (1986, pp 36–7) and some from the REC (2013b, pp 16–23).

Relational RE

Mastery learning in RE has many components, including the ability to build relationships and connections in learning. Cooling, Bessant and Key show how the brain is wired to connect, maintaining that it requires to know something of the bigger picture to contextualize and establish learning. They advocate giving the pupils some pre-exposure to study material so that the brain knows where to go next and so that the patterns connect. They suggest giving the pupils a copy of a topic mind map, maintaining that 'The brain likes to have the big picture first and details, second' (http://www.rethinking.co.uk). The writers provide an example of such a map, and choose the church as the main concept. Around this title are written the associated key concepts on thick branches which then lead to more detail on sub-branches, which in turn lead to their own sub-branches as greater detail is developed with the pupils' ideas included. The leading concepts they associate with church are ministry, people, worship and building, and these in turn lead to around seventy associated ideas/concepts. Cooling et al. rationalize the use of such a mind map:

> Teachers need to organise material to reveal the pattern that is present in an RE topic. It may not be obvious to pupils that the stories of Joseph, the prodigal son and Jonah are all about forgiveness.
>
> (http://www.rethinking.co.uk)

Task six: Make a mind map

Choose one of the following or one of your choosing and construct a concept map. Think about how you might construct this with the pupils and incorporate their ideas.

- Jewish worship
- Hindu puja and Arti
- The Golden Rule
- The relationship between belief and action in Islam
- Rules and precepts in Buddhism
- Community and the Khalsa

Use the mind map to begin to plan teaching and learning for a six-week RE topic for an age of your choosing.

Task seven: Relational RE

So, continuing the idea of building connections, it could be argued that effective teaching in RE draws on relationships as one idea flows from another.

How important do you think the following links are for effective RE? Consider each one and how you would ensure that these links are made in planning for effective RE. What would your classroom look like if these relationships were forged?

- teacher with pupil – based on trust, understanding and non-coercion,
- pupil with pupil – learning to speak and listen with respect and attention,
- new learning with prior learning and future learning – appreciating the big picture,
- the use of resources related to the main concepts being learned,
- tasks and assessment for the lesson with the main learning objectives,
- pupils' experiences and the RE material,
- homework tasks and the main conceptual frameworks,
- religious teachings and practice,
- RE material and deeper theology/meaning,
- the mind, body and spirit in holistic forms of teaching and learning,
- explicit and implicit forms of RE,
- RE and other curriculum subjects.

Ninian Smart (1973, pp 42–3) noted seven dimensions of religion that can largely be seen to be integrated, interconnected and synthetic rather than separate. As Stern points out, these dimensions underpin a phenomenological approach to study so that 'Learning in RE is focused upon assembling, broadening and deepening understanding that takes religion's phenomena on its own terms' (Stern 2018a, p 67). The dimensions are

- practical and ritual,
- experiential and emotional,
- narrative and mythical,
- doctrinal and philosophical,
- social and institutional,
- material and artistic and
- ethical and legal.

These seven are facets of the way people use belief and practice to make sense of life and living. Smart's thinking supports a connected epistemological view of religion. Understanding religion as made up of these aspects will help pupils build up a holistic picture of worldviews.

How can using enquiry skills develop pupils' autonomy and agency?

Enquiry-based learning can develop pupils' sense of autonomy and agency as they construct their own questions and focus of enquiry. Teachers often think that high-achieving pupils prefer to organize and execute their own research topics, but all pupils can develop skills through conducting enquiries. Pupils will need to work collaboratively, learning essential life skills. They will need to work together to find supportive evidence, connect their resulting explanations and provisional answers to knowledge gained through their investigations and create an argument in defence of their hypothesis or thinking. Such learning is well situated to collaborative group work, and is sympathetic to the dynamics of community that is at the heart of religion and belief. For example, the church is often thought to refer to the building itself, whereas Jesus spoke about it as being the body (corpus) of people who share faith. Gates notes the following:

> There is much in contemporary western culture which takes as unquestionable norm that the goal of education is human autonomy. Enabling each pupil to think for themselves becomes the overarching goal of every curriculum subject. ... However, the cultivation of the individual can have very isolating outcomes, which are at the expense of other relatedness and relational belonging. The 'I' is supreme, but entirely solitary.
>
> (Gates, in Broadbent and Brown 2002, p 109)

So as pupils join in a community of enquiry, a suitable pattern for group work might be in this form:

- Decide on a question that comes from our topic.
- Choose some methods of finding out some answers to your question.
- Search for some books or the internet or talk to some people to help you.
- Collect and analyse/sort the data and choose which is best to deal with your enquiry.
- See what the data are telling you.
- Order your argument and see what you now know that you didn't know before.
- Tell the other pupils and your teacher what you have discovered.
- Decide the best ways that will help them to learn from you.
- Decide where your research may now lead your group in a new enquiry.

This approach to finding out can be seen to be sympathetic with the principles and philosophy underpinning the Philosophy for Children movement (P4C). According to their website (https://p4c.com), P4C encourages children to explore ideas without the fear of being right or wrong while they learn that their ideas and the ideas of others have value. So children learn to dialogue in respect. The process advocated begins with a stimulus and the children are expected to decide, collaboratively, on a 'I wonder why …' question to follow up. This can then lead to 'What if' styles of learning (see http://www.whatiflearning.co.uk/). Some teachers might be wary of adopting an open learning style in RE because it is thought that while philosophy asks questions and teaches pupils to dialogue, religion seeks to provide answers and can view questioning as doubt or rejection. However, an important task of the teacher in enquiry-based learning is to be a contributor to discussion rather than positioned as expert. The teacher's task is to facilitate discussion that is not stifled but free and exploratory. There are some excellent ideas to promote thinking skills detailed by Cooling (http://www.rethinking.co.uk).

Some enquiries that have been used effectively in school are the following:

- What are the main Christian symbols and what do they mean?
- What do Hindus and Sikhs say about how the world came to be?
- How do different religions use colour in their worship?
- What do Humanists believe it is to be a good citizen?
- How do different religions and non-religious worldviews use candles in worship and celebration?

In one school, Year 5 investigated how religious and non-religious people learn to follow the Golden Rule and began by compiling a charter of how they would like to be treated by others. They used this as the basis for the golden rules of the classroom. They looked at the different rights of pupils and decided that to be loved was one of the most important. They considered what 1 Corinthians 13 from the New Testament of the Christian Bible says about love and sought to express this through art, drama, music, poetry and calligram. They found stories and accounts of those who showed love to others from religious and non-religious backgrounds. They then looked at some of the following teachings to see how different religions and worldviews teach about the Golden Rule.

- Always treat others as you would like them to treat you (Matthew 7:12, Christianity).
- Base conduct on simple, humane principles and commit yourself to active citizenship (Ronald Fletcher, Humanism).
- Hurt not others with that which pains yourself (Buddhism, Samyutta Nikaya V. 353).
- As thou deemest thyself, so deem others (Sikhism, Kabir).

- What is hateful to you, do not do to your fellow man (Judaism, Talmud: Shabbat 31a).
- No one of you is a believer until he loves for his brother what he loves for himself (Islam, Forty Hadith of an-Nawawi 13).
- Do not to others what if done to you would cause you pain (Hinduism, Mahabharata Anusasana Parva 113.8).

The pupils considered why the rule is called 'Golden' and made up a silver and bronze rule.

Task eight: Your own research

In preparation for teaching the pupils how to research, conduct a piece of research about your own RE practice. Choose an area that you think will help you improve or that you think you will struggle with or that you presently worry about. Perhaps something like one of these:

- How can I live my educational value of respect for all in RE?
- How can I ensure that I teach difficult concepts in age-appropriate ways?
- How will I be able to know all I need to in order to teach RE effectively?
- How can I ensure that I provide opportunities for spiritual development in my RE?

Tell someone else what you are doing and ensure that you share your research findings with others. Sharing can really focus the mind. Remember that the pupils, too, need to see a reason for their research and, like adults, will learn more thoroughly if they know they must teach or present their material to an audience. In linking research with practice and sharing your findings, you are ensuring that it will have impact, for you and potentially for others.

When you have completed Task Eight, you might want to think about how it complements the various tasks in this book where you are investigating the ideas of the pupils you teach – such as Task Three in this chapter, and most of the activities in Chapter 6.

As Chapter 5 closes and as you seek to improve your practice and grasp what effective RE is, considering what Blaylock has to say might be helpful:

- Good RE engages with aspects of the whole of religion but is clear about the particular standpoints.
- Good RE is alert to the contemporary as well as the historical of religion.
- Good RE is positive about religion and its treasures but covers the negative too whilst avoiding stereotypes.

- Good RE is not representative – it never says the study is finished so is tentative and partial but 'those patches of a religion that can be examined are approached in depth, both critically and empathetically'.

- 'Good RE does not exist without the careful planning and development of some teacher expertise.'

- Good RE is willing to be personal – 'there is no such thing as Buddhism, just a lot of people who are Buddhists'.

- Good RE teachers can make a difference by 'opening windows into faith from classrooms in ways that seek integrity'.

(Blaylock 2004, p 62)

Summary

This chapter has emphasized the need for RE to be a thoughtful subject that encourages pupils to think critically. In learning to think for themselves they will be able to weigh up what they think about the claims of different worldviews and religions. Researching different aspects should empower them and provide them with a greater sense of autonomy and agency. Are you ready for the pupils you will teach to do this? RE that encompasses this methodology and pedagogy will be risky and challenging, but the alternative is not viable. How willing are you to consider the ultimate questions of life and living and how thoughtful are you as a teacher of the subject? You should not ask others to do what you are not willing to do yourself. That is challenging for the teacher.

Recommended reading

Blaylock, L (ed) (2004) *Representing Religions*; Birmingham: Christian Education.

Hull, J M (1991) *God-Talk with Young Children: Notes for Parents and Teachers*; London: Continuum.

Stern, L J (2018a) *Teaching Religious Education: Researchers in the Classroom: Second Edition*; London: Bloomsbury.

Chapter 6
Children's Ideas – Promoting Curiosity

Chapter objectives

- What are the ideas that pupils bring to RE and how are they formed?
- How can teachers find out about pupils' ideas?
- Why is it important to know about and work with pupils' ideas?
- Taking the experiences of pupils seriously
- How can teachers find out about pupils' ideas? Using dialogue in irresistible RE
- Learning how to listen and speak in RE including conflict
- How can pupils develop spiritually, morally, socially and culturally in effective RE?

Introduction

If we want pupils to be curious, we need to be curious ourselves as teachers. RE can be a daunting subject to teach, because it is such a huge subject filled with ideas and information that are unfamiliar to most adults. This chapter makes a virtue out of this necessity. We *have* to be curious when we teach RE, because there is no way we can simply know everything. And the starting point for the curiosity of teachers is being curious about – and trying to understand – what the pupils know. That is the starting point for this chapter.

What are the ideas that pupils bring to RE and how are they formed?

Pupils will bring many ideas into the classroom about the topics covered by RE. They get their ideas from their families and friends, from the television and other media, and they will think through ideas on their own. Some will be used to working with and interacting with religious ideas and worldviews. These pupils may practice religion at home and in places of worship, and they may be religiously literate. Others will be unfamiliar with religion or other worldviews, although they will still have thought about some RE issues – the life-and-death issues, the issues of right and wrong or of fairness and justice. Whatever the pupils bring with them, they come to the classroom curious and with minds well suited to engage with the ideas RE has to offer. So, many children will have encountered the story of the Good Samaritan and from a young age understand that this is an account of helping others irrespective of creed or colour: at school, in the family and wider community, as this display shows (Figure 6.1).

Figure 6.1 The Good Samaritan, by St Mary and St Thomas Aquinas Catholic Primary School, Gateshead

Look at the sense of justice in the following (Figure 6.2):

The Bus Ride That Changed History

I chose this title because the picture dates back to when Rosa Parks had the courage to say 'No' this made me think about when Black people were separated from the whites.

In my picture you can see Rosa Parks at the back of the bus and the whites at the front. I've tried to recreate the bus using different types of materials.

When I was making my picture I felt sad that everyone was not able to live a happy life because everyone was split up. I don't think it was right and I would have said 'No' like Rosa Park.

Children feel strongly about such matters. A Year 5 group of pupils looked at the image *The Angry Christ* by Lino Pontebon – an unusual image. The teacher linked

Figure 6.2 The bus ride that changed history, by Erica (age ten), Leicester Grammar Junior School

the image with the account of Jesus clearing the temple in Mark Chapter 11. The pupils discussed why he was angry and whether anger is always wrong. They talked about the difference between anger and temper and about the things that made them see red. There are some very good ideas supplied by the Barnabus Trust (http://www.barnabasinschools.org.uk/) for extending this lesson.

The pupils looked up Amos 5:15 and 24 in the Old Testament and thought about how God wants people to act fairly. How God says that being fair should tumble out of people like water from a waterfall, and doing what's right should be like a stream that never stops flowing.

They then thought about what sort of actions could be included in a 'stream of fairness' or a 'waterfall of justice' and created their own image to show this.

Although this example is based on the Bible and is taken from the Christian perspective, you might like to think how to teach this lesson from a Humanist perspective. Humanism might be summed up in the following that has been written by one Humanist group: good without God; morals without religion; rites without religion; ceremonies without superstition and ethical atheism. Older pupils could discuss what these mean and design collages or posters to illustrate the slogans.

What pupils are *not* are 'blank slates'. By the age of four or five, pupils will have learned more than they will ever learn during the rest of their lives. They will have done this by watching and listening to everything that happens around them, and by trying out their own ideas and actions. From the moment they are born, pupils are interacting with people and objects. Studies of babies just a few hours old suggest that they can tell the difference between having a live 'conversation' (of facial expressions and baby talk) with their mother via a video link, and watching a video of their mother making all the same expressions and noises. The video – when the baby and mother are not in a live conversation – is of little interest to the baby. Babies crave dialogue right from the start of their lives. (Twins start their relationships with each other even before they are born.)

Once pupils get to an age to attend school, they are buzzing with ideas, full of questions and answers – some right, some wrong (and some that are both right and wrong, perhaps). The teacher's job is not to write lots of facts on the pupil's 'blank slate' brain, but to *add to* and *guide* the pupil's ideas and knowledge. Think of the pupils as already four or five years into a wonderful journey: you are lucky enough to be joining their journey and introducing them to all kinds of new adventures, but the journey was under way long before you met them and will continue long after they leave you. Just try to make your part of their journey as interesting and valuable as you can. For some pupils this may be a pilgrimage to religious ortho-doxy, for some, a rejection of this, for others they may be on a threshold of faith. But for all, they are on a personal quest in coming to know what they think and believe. It is the teacher's task to accompany and dialogue with them throughout the journey.

One pupil says this:

Journey of faith (Figure 6.3)

'Art in Heaven' work is about disciples going on a spiritual journey to re-ignite their faith. This art work is spiritual because we have been learning about pilgrimage in RE.

In my picture you can see thousands of disciples being drawn to their places of worship. Doing this work has made me think about how pilgrims play a big part of different faiths.

A quote from a holy book that fits with my work is … 'I come to you Lord for protection: never let me be defeated. You are a righteous God. Save me I pray' (Psalms 31). I think this means that God is always with us and will protect us through good and bad.

The Afghan Muslim poet Rumi wrote, in the thirteenth century, of 'two kinds of intelligence'. One kind is acquired through memorization, and is useful in helping you 'rise in the world' and gain rank. The other is 'fresh' and 'fluid' and is 'a foun-tainhead from within you, moving out' (Rumi 1995, p 178). Both are important, but some teachers all too easily concentrate only on the memorization that will help gain rank in the world, and fail to notice what the child brings. That is the reason for this chapter.

How can teachers find out about pupils' ideas?

Pupils should be asked for their views, what they think and what they know. This seems so obvious, and so straightforward, that you may think it not worth men-

Figure 6.3 Journey of faith, by Alyssa (aged ten), of Canon Burrows CE Primary School, Ashton-under-Lyne

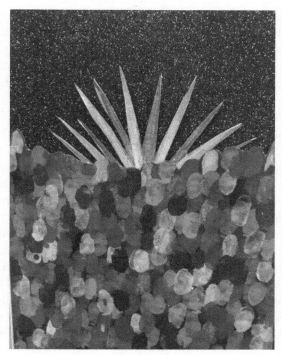

tioning. However, when an adult (especially a teacher) asks a question of pupils, the pupils will usually first try to work out what you want to hear. The same is true of adults, of course. You might be asked the question 'how are you?' by your doctor, by your best friend or by a colleague as you pass each other in the corridor. Your answer is likely to be different, depending on who is asking. It is to be hoped that you give your doctor a very different answer to the answer you would give to your colleague, and when your friend asks the question, your answer might be anything – depending on the situation you find yourselves in. Children are just the same. So when you ask a question of a pupil in school, the pupil's first thought is usually 'what does this teacher want me to say?' After all, pupils want to be polite (most of the time) and want to please their teachers (most of the time).

The difficulty with finding out what pupils think is well illustrated by some research by Jeffcoate (described by Carrington and Troyna 1988). Pupils aged four were asked by their teacher to 'discuss pictures portraying black people in ... a variety of situations' and the pupils' discussions (with teachers present) were all appropriate and 'could not possibly be construed as racially offensive'. However, the pictures were then left 'casually' around the classroom (close to hidden recording devices), and 'the comments made by the pupils, in the assumed absence of an adult audience, were undeniably racist in tenor' (Carrington and Troyna 1988, p 21).

There are different ways of interpreting this research, but what seems clear is that the pupils – already, at the age of only four – knew exactly when they 'could' and 'couldn't' (or 'should' and 'shouldn't') be racist.

If four-year-olds know what teachers want to hear, and are happy to tell them what they want to hear, then the rest of primary education won't get any easier. Primary teachers need to be aware of this, but it creates a real dilemma. All teachers want and need to be good role models to the pupils they teach, and one of the ways this is done is by pupils seeking to emulate their teachers. Lawrence-Lightfoot has referred to this as teachers being 'society's professional adults' (Lawrence-Lightfoot 2003, p xxi). But if teachers are good role models, then how do teachers enable pupils to tell them things that the pupils will know might be contrary to the teachers' beliefs? One way of doing this is for teachers to model openness and uncertainty. Being a good role model includes modelling getting things wrong, misunderstanding things, realizing that your views may be very different to those of other (good) people, sincerely admitting you are sorry, and much more. If pupils think their teachers are perfect (because teachers pretend to be perfect), then this is not healthy. Instead, pupils need teachers who – of course – are trying to be caring and curious and fair and much more, and who are *also* at least a little bit uncertain. The RE writer Durka describes the 'learned uncertainty of teachers' (Durka 2002, p 1). This could be described as the virtue of 'humility'. Some people are uncomfortable with being humble, as it can seem deferential and unassertive – qualities that teachers may think unhelpful in the classroom. So the virtue of 'learned uncertainty' may appeal more. There are many religious traditions of humility (e.g. in the Christian tradition) and uncertainty (e.g. in the Zen Buddhist tradition), so teachers of RE can even make a lesson out of their humility/uncertainty. Pupils may then learn from their teachers that being a 'professional adult' includes uncertainty and mistakes – and being open about these qualities. Then, perhaps, pupils will be more willing to express their own views, and to discuss them honestly with their teachers.

Being open to new ideas is, incidentally, one of the qualities most needed by researchers. If researchers simply find out what they thought they would find out, it is likely that the research is a failure. The best research surprises the researcher. This researcher-attitude is good for teachers, too. Let the pupils surprise you, and you will be educating them. As the Jewish philosopher Buber said, 'a real lesson … that is, neither a routine repetition nor a lesson whose findings the teacher knows before he starts, … [is] one which develops in mutual surprises' (Buber 2002, p 241). Teaching RE is a good lesson in uncertainty anyway, as the subject – covering most of the world's history and culture and belief and practice – is so vast, no one could possibly know more than a tiny bit of the subject matter. Teachers can turn that problem into an opportunity, and celebrate their roles as *uncertain but curious*. As an example, many teachers in primary and secondary schools teach RE lessons about death. Often, these will involve explaining to pupils that, for example, Christians generally believe in heaven (and perhaps hell), Hindus have reincarnation, atheists tend to believe death is the end and so on. A questionnaire was carried out in 1997 (see Fageant and Blaylock 1998, Blaylock 2001, Weston 2003 and http://old.natre.org.uk/db/). It asked pupils aged seven to eighteen many things including what they thought would happen to them when they die. The pupils' responses were fascinating. Here are four examples from eleven-year-olds (with the spelling retained as originally written):

> I think that death is just a place you have to go back to. Everyone is going to go there weather they like it or not.
>
> I dont think there is such thing as an afterlife and when we die we are dead and that is the end of us but if we are murdered we turn into spirits.
>
> You go to a church to have a cermoney and people cry. You get beried and get eaton by maggots or over animals. You get to sleep and be peaceful.
>
> I afraid of death but part of me want's to die.

Task one: Surprised?

What surprises you in the four responses to the question above about death?

When other people have read them, they sometimes say that the surprise was not simply that these views were 'correct' or 'incorrect' (according to the pupils' own reported religious or non-religious allegiances), or that they were sophisticated or philosophically interesting responses (even if they often were). The bigger surprise is often that the pupils seemed to have such strong, deeply felt, personal views. Teaching pupils a 'list' of what members of different religious groups might believe is still interesting, but it is unlikely to be as surprising – or important – as asking what pupils themselves believe, in an atmosphere where they feel comfortable telling teachers what they really think. A researcher is someone who is curious – genuinely curious, and wanting to be surprised – and this piece of research from 1997 is a good example of how a research attitude can surprise researchers and teachers alike.

Describe some of the surprises you have already had about the pupils you have seen when in schools. (These may be related to any subject of the curriculum.) In what ways has your thinking changed, as a result of those surprises? In what ways will you act differently as a teacher, as a result of those surprises? Describe some ways that you will surprise your pupils in RE.

The same questionnaire also asked pupils what they liked about RE. Here are some of their answers (with their ages in years in brackets):

- I do like parts of RE like when I talk about who I am. [ten]
- Most of the time when we do RE I don't know its RE so but I do enjoy it because it tells us about different religions. [ten]
- Yes, B because I like learning about different people and the way they live. [ten]
- I don't usually like this work because I think R.E's a bit like History which I don't take like. [ten]

- Some bits I enjoy, some bits I don't. I Find it interesting to find out about other religions. [nine]

- I like some stories from the bible even though I don't believe them. [eleven]

- I enjoy these bits of school yes, because its part of our education but R.E. is good because it's like a private time to write what you think not what anybody else thincks. [ten]

- I don't really belive in all those god's but I enjoy learning about them because it is very interesting and I learn alot about it. [nine]

- I ~~engay~~ engoyed it when I lernt about buddaha. Because my mum belevs in buddha. [nine]

- I like learning about god and Jesus. I like listening to stories. [nine]

- I enjoy learning about other peoples religions and I think it is important that we don't just learn about religion. [ten]

- Yes I enjoy these bit's of school. I like it because it is interesting. What I like about R.E. is it's history and I like history. [nine]

- I like the way you can ~~follow~~ learn to follow Jesus and his rules. I like the way you can ~~learn~~ decide weather you want to follow Jesus. [nine]

- I dont like RE but I think it's educational. [ten]

- You find out the past and the future rolled into one. And it really makes me think and sometimes wonder if these people are real or made up? [ten]

Task two: Do you have to like RE?

Having read the list of RE 'likes' and 'dislikes' supplied by pupils, imagine they were all your pupils. Which comments would you be most proud of? Which comments would make you want to change how you teach RE? (How would you change?)

Why is it important to know about and work with pupils' ideas?

It is vital to work with pupils' ideas in RE because they are brilliant and original thinkers. Picture this true account of a seven-year-old pupil making connections. A teacher is considering the Jewish and Christian narrative of Abraham being prepared to sacrifice his son in obedience to what God asks him to do to test his faith. You can read the account in Genesis Chapter 2. (In Islam a similar story is recounted, but it is Ishmael not Isaac who is to be the victim: you can read this in the Qur'an Sura 37 'The Ranged', with more detail in later documents.) As the narrative comes to the end, the teacher asks the pupils if they have any questions or observations. One pupil raises his hand and says the following:

That reminds me of another story. Jesus had to carry his own cross like Isaac helped with the wood for the fire. His dad was ready to give up his son even though it was hard to do. It's just different where Jesus actually died and Isaac didn't.

This pupil was making the kind of connections that learned theologians make. Many Christians believe that everything in the Hebrew Bible points towards the coming of and salvific work of Christ. Pupils can make these connections and often will, if and when they are presented with the big pictures of religion rather than fragmented snippets. These puzzles and mysteries of connection call on the highest thinking and creative skills a pupil possesses.

Maria James researched primary pupils' concepts of God, asking them – among other things – to draw, write about and talk about their ideas about God. There are many interesting findings from the research, including the finding that pupils' ideas about God tended to be more complex and sophisticated in their writing, compared to their drawing, and even more complex and sophisticated in their speaking. One activity that can be developed from that research asked pupils to describe the 'job' that God does. Here is a task for you, based on one pupil's response.

Task three: Concepts of God

Look at the following snippets from *God's Job*, written by Danny aged eight:

- One of God's jobs is making people. He makes them to replace the ones that die so that there will be enough people to take care of things on earth. God's second job is listening to people's prayers an awful lot of this goes on, since some people like preachers and things, pray at times besides bedtimes. God sees everything and hears everything and is everywhere which keeps him pretty busy. So you shouldn't go wasting his time by going over your parents' head asking for something they said you couldn't have. Atheists are people who don't believe in God.

- Jesus is God's son he used to do all the hard work like walking on water and performing miracles and trying to teach the people who didn't want to learn about God they finally got tired of him preaching to them and they crucified him. But he was good and kind like his father and he told his father that they didn't know what they were doing and to forgive them.

- God told him he could stay in heaven. And now he helps his dad out by listening to prayers and seeing to things that are important to God to take care of and which ones he can take care of himself without having to bother God.

In these quotations, the writing has been corrected a little, but the theological views expressed by Danny are impressive by any standards.

What would you write at the end of Danny's piece of work?

Taking the experiences of pupils seriously

In recent research (Stern and Shillitoe 2018), a questionnaire was given to pupils aged seven to sixteen, and it included a question about their religion or worldview. There was a list given, which included Buddhist, Christian, Hindu, Jewish, Muslim, Sikh, agnostic, atheist, Humanist, spiritual but not religious and prefer not to say. Then there was a box with 'Other (please state)'. The researchers had tried to cover most of the expected responses in the long initial list. What surprised them was the number of pupils who filled in the 'Other (please state)' box. Among these 'other' categories were the following:

- ~~Atheist~~ actually, I don't know whether to believe it or not.
- Baptised a Christian but gradually morphed into a Humanist/Agnostic
- Buddhist and Christian
- Catholic because I was baptised but I dont believe in God or any God. I'm a person who doesn't believe of any of it
- Don't know yet
- Either Christian or Muslim
- Half Christian (not christened)
- I follow some of the Buddhist principals but not religious
- In the middle of believing in god and not believing
- Jewish by blood, Atheist by belief
- Spiritual but not religious / only believe in some things religious

The pupils in your classes will probably be like the pupils who responded to that questionnaire. You may have confidently self-identified Christians, Jews, Muslims, atheists and so on, and you may have a group of pupils who – like the 'other' categories described here – are sitting between groups, or who are conscious of changing over time. This is a gloriously mixed group of people to work with on RE. Most teachers do not know the details of the religious or non-religious beliefs of their pupils, and RE teachers should not be pushing pupils to 'confess' their views – and should not feel obliged to confess their own views, either. Sometimes a pupil will be embarrassed to describe their position if it is different to the views of their own family, if it is different to the views of their teachers or if it is different to the views of their fellow pupils – and potentially the source of bullying. Sometimes a pupil simply wants to maintain privacy on this topic. But of course the pupils (and their teachers) make for wonderful resources, whether or not they talk about their own beliefs. Taking the views of pupils seriously therefore means accepting the likely range of pupil positions *and* the likely range of attitudes to telling you about their positions. It also means listening carefully to what they have to say.

Suppose you have some pupils in your class who describe themselves as Jewish, and who are known to the other pupils as Jewish. Clive Lawton describes his

own schooldays as a Jew in mid-twentieth-century England (e.g. at http://www.bbc.
co.uk/religion/religions/judaism/beliefs/eyes_1.shtml). He describes how Jewish are
the stories told of Jesus, although he was himself restricted to off-stage roles in the
annual Nativity plays. (In many Christian picture books, the only biblical characters
to be portrayed looking Jewish – often in a stereotyped way – are the 'baddies' such
as King Herod or Judas Iscariot.) Lawton also describes how puzzled he was when he
heard descriptions of Judaism in school, as they didn't match his own understanding.
This all means we need to listen carefully. There will undoubtedly be Jewish pupils
in your class who realize the importance of the home as a place for worship and the
part their mothers play in this, and who are aware of how rules and traditions allow
family members to know their unique place and what God requires of them. They
may celebrate Shabbat and take from this an understanding of the concept of rest and
reflection, and they may know how the festivals are linked to the stories found in the
Torah brought to life in celebration and community. They may know some Hebrew.
Teachers will find pupils who can confidently talk about such issues a really valuable
resource. However, teachers must also recognize that, perhaps, *the Jewish pupils do
not know any of this*.

The best teachers will be excited to discover what their pupils already know so
that they are aware of what they are building upon. They will also be excited to
know what remains to be learned. This means we do not simply assume a Jewish or
Christian or atheist pupil knows a lot about Judaism or Christianity or atheism, any
more than a pupil from England will know much English history, or, for that matter,
a pupil who is a human being will know about the biology of human beings. Pupils
need to know that their ideas matter, and so they need and deserve to be listened to.
Yet from the moment they can talk, pupils may have been told to listen. This is sadly
most often the case in school. Pupils often describe a 'proper' lesson as one in which
the teacher talks and the pupils listen. Teacher = talker. Pupil = listener. These are
the first equations most pupils learn. Try it the other way around: teacher = listener;
pupil = talker. Perhaps it is easier to describe in another way. In classical music, the
most important person in an orchestra (the person who gets most money, and whose
name is biggest in the publicity material) is the conductor. (This is also often true
of a music producer or a DJ, in much chart and club music.) What does a classical
conductor and a record producer sound like? Both of them are silent: their job is
listening. It is the musicians – the violinists or flautists, the singers or instrumental-
ists – who make the noise. But the conductor or producer gets the best out of their
musicians, and rightly deserves credit for this. As a teacher, you will need to talk and
to 'perform', and this may help you survive as a teacher. But it is your 'listening'
persona that will make you a *great* teacher, a teacher who is mastering RE and all the
other subjects. You will be listening, even when you are talking. You will be watching
the pupils to see if they are really interested in what you say, or just being polite – just
as they will notice whether you are really interested in what they say.

Pupils need and demand to be listened to. However, as Cat Stevens/Yusuf
Islam sings, 'from the moment I could talk I was ordered to listen' (from his song
Father and Son, Cat Stevens, 1970). We can all draw up images when pupils crave

to be heard but have been shunned by overly busy adults. *Not Now, Bernard* (McKee 1980) is one of the best stories for young pupils that show how they feel about not being heard. (Spoiler alert: Bernard ends up being eaten by, or becoming, a monster.) We have observed teaching sessions which have gone awry because the teacher has not given the pupils space to say what they think or to compose the questions they want answered. What can be even worse is when teachers think they are listening to pupils but they are really just getting the pupils to guess what they want to hear. Listening – listening so hard that pupils say what they really think – is much harder than it seems.

How can teachers find out about pupils' ideas? Using dialogue in irresistible RE

As the previous section explains, it is much harder finding out what pupils think than it seems at first. How do teachers find out about pupils' ideas?

- Teachers should talk *with* pupils rather than *at* them, and should be listening with real interest to what pupils have to say.

- Teachers should use open-ended questions that have no easy, straightforward answers. (Religions and non-religious worldviews rarely have easy, straight-forward answers to the important questions, either.)

- Teachers should demonstrate, in what they do with pupils, that asking puzzling questions, and trying to work out answers to such questions, is a good thing to do and an exciting way of living. If preparing pupils for SATs is getting you down, remember, *curiosity killed the SAT* (Stern 2018b).

- Teachers should demonstrate that knowledge and the quest for wisdom and truth is an inexhaustible task, a journey that never ends. Never-ending journeys are the ones most like life itself.

Stern notes that 'dialogue has been central to religious and educational traditions for thousands of years, yet many people associate religion with authoritative mono-logue (such as in stereotypes of endless sermonising), so the importance of dialogue needs stressing' (Stern 2018a, p 9). So, even though dialogue has been central to religious traditions, many people have had the experience of religious communities being reluctant to engage with dialogue. This is the same situation that teachers find themselves in. It is a profession that is essentially dialogic (as described by Alexander 2004, 2006), but too often teachers are monologic. The best RE teaching takes the teachings and practices of the religions and non-religious worldviews represented in Great Britain and asks 'So what?' The process becomes a dialogue, a dialogue with the traditions *and* a dialogue with the pupils. What relevance and meaning can the pupils draw from these traditions for their own spiritual, moral, social and cultural development? Religious and non-religious material is presented in a way that opens up dialogue. Teachers encourage investigation of what it means to be a Jew, a Sikh, a Humanist, and they take the opportunity for pupils to develop their own ways of making sense of the world and their place within it.

The 2013 RE review noted that RE 'should develop in pupils an aptitude for dialogue so that they can participate positively in our society with its diverse religions and worldviews' (REC 2013a, p 14). This is a call for pupils to participate in dialogue. Meanwhile, pupils are – too often – expected to guess the answer the teacher expects. Ahlberg's poem *The Answer* (Ahlberg 1991) describes beautifully the frustration of pupils trying to find the 'right answer' when it is hidden in the teacher's head. This is a good poem to read to pupils, to show them the difference between thinking deeply about a question for themselves and simply trying to work out what the teacher is thinking.

Task four: Where is the answer?

Read Ahlberg's poem *The Answer* to a class of pupils. Get them to give you examples from their own school of when they have had to guess what the teacher is thinking, like in the poem.

Now, ask them an interesting, difficult question from the RE syllabus. Tell them that your head is empty, and they will have to find the answer inside their own heads.

When they have thought of some answers and have shared these answers around the class, ask them what the differences are between answering a question by trying to find the answer hidden in the teacher's head and trying to find the answer in their *own* heads.

Learning how to listen and speak in RE including conflict

We should listen to pupils in RE because they have things to teach us. Read (and really 'listen to') the following (Figure 6.4):

The Art of Equality

In our picture, we are expressing the equality between men and women and how our religion shouldn't be sexist. Our picture shows that equality brings joy to the world; it will make its better place for people to live in with less abuse to women and more rights. In our piece of art, when the God and the Goddess touch freedom and elation break out in the world. Every animal follows to the freedom and elation of the earth; for we think that animals should have the same respect as we do and less cruelty in their lives (being stored in restricted, squalid areas). We have considered that nature brings colour as well as happiness, meaning we shouldn't be polluting and damaging our delicate world, like people are committing this action as you read this. To make our art, what has inspired us is, what would happen if both genders were equal? For this project we hope our art will remind people that both genders should be equal and one gender not better than the other.

Figure 6.4 The art of equality, by Alexandra and Esme (aged eleven), St Mary's CE Primary School

Learning to listen and speak are essential skills to learn in RE, so that pupils can come to their own way of thinking. However, some teachers are anxious about opening up dialogical space because they are worried that conflicts and sensitivities might arise from what the pupils bring from home and from what they have heard. This is an understandable anxiety, and teachers should be aware of these sensitivities. But it is an *unavoidable* anxiety. Taking all conflicts out of RE would be like taking numbers out of mathematics or taking dates out of history. Something would be left, but it would be of much less value. Conflict is central to religions and non-religious traditions – conflict *within* as well as *between* these traditions. As a teacher of RE, you will need to deal with some of these conflicts, but you will not be able to solve them all. Dialogue between different positions helps create understanding on both sides. A competitive debate with winners and losers is less likely to create understanding. As Knauth describes it,

> Conflict is not … the opposite of dialogue. Conflict, rather, is necessarily incorporated in the concept of dialogue, which relies on different, partly conflicting perspectives. To bring these different and conflicting perspectives into a communicative exchange is one of the central aims of the assumed notion of dialogue. This does not mean harmonising and levelling out differences, but rather bridging them, in order to foster a living together in diversity. Conflict, thus, is the practical test of living together.
>
> (Knauth, in Avest et al. 2009, pp 111–12)

This might sound an ambitious aspiration for the primary RE classroom, but if pupils do not learn to appreciate difference here, a valuable opportunity can be lost. Some of the best teaching and learning sessions in RE that we have witnessed have been those where the teacher speaks minimally. As the pupils' views and evolving knowledge are taken seriously, their self-esteem improves and they begin to realize themselves as capable knowers who can articulate their own views. Of course there must be times for more didactic forms of teaching to communicate factual information, and to provide context and impetus for discussion. However, as Kincheloe shows, this needs to lead to a 'terrain of discomfort where knowledge is too complex to simply give it out for use on multiple choice texts or convergent questions' (Kincheloe 2008, p 111). In this case, even young pupils can recognize the complexity of the lived world and they are more likely to learn to live with the puzzling questions that both religions and non-religious worldviews pose.

As teachers develop more dialogical teaching strategies for the classroom, it is exhilarating when real, unforced conversations take place, and ideas dance together. It is significant that the writers of the *Cambridge Primary Review* state that 'enacting dialogue' should be one of the twelve core aims of the curriculum. They advocate helping pupils grasp the notion that knowledge is negotiated and created. Further, they note that 'Dialogue is central to pedagogy: between self and others, between personal and collective knowledge, between present and past, between different ways of thinking' (Alexander 2009, p 19). Alexander defines dialogue as 'achieving common understanding through structured, cumulative questioning and discussion which guide and prompt, reduce choices, minimise risk and error, and expedite "handover" of concepts and principles' (Alexander 2006, p 30). He stresses that what learners say needs to be taken seriously: their utterances 'need to be reflected upon, discussed, even argued about' (Alexander 2006, p 27). Knowledge that is constructed through dialogue between the teacher and pupils is inexhaustible.

> There is neither a first nor a last word and there are no limits to the dialogic context (it extends into the boundless past and boundless future). Even past meanings, that is those born in the dialogue of past centuries, can never be stable (finalized, ended once and for all) – they will always change (be renewed) in the process of subsequent, future development of the dialogue.
>
> (Bakhtin 1986, p 170)

Alexander identifies teaching as negotiation, a mode that enacts 'the democratic principle in teaching; seeing knowledge as fluid rather than fixed, created afresh rather than handed down; creating teachers and pupils as joint enquirers' (Alexander 2006, p 29). He argues that transmissive pedagogies, conversely, 'are based on a view of knowledge as given, propositional and fixed' (Alexander 2006, p 32). Alexander also led a review of the whole primary curriculum (Alexander 2010), which followed many of these principles.

Trainee students that we have known have enjoyed discussing in their RE sessions in university. Nicola and Laura point out that this is an important stimulus for building dialogical space in their classrooms.

> I think teaching RE will give me a chance to undertake very interesting debates in the classroom like the ones we have had. This will enable me to get to know the children and what matters to them in a way other subjects may not.
>
> (Nicola, PGCE Student)

> I felt we could express our opinions on the subject of religion freely without being discouraged or negative comments being frowned upon. This means that I will be able to manage talk more in my classroom as I feel more confident not to always have the right answers.
>
> (Laura, PGCE Student)

Many people find dialogue in RE worrying. Talk of religion, with its implications for experiences of living and dying and discussion of ultimate questions of life, can be searching and exacting. When we regard teaching as dialogue between the knowers and the material, it is easier to rethink our own roles.

> It becomes clearer that we are to create a space in which truth is neither suppressed nor merely accepted. The focus is not on instant answers but rather on adventure, wrestling with untruth, silence and listening.
>
> (Durka 2002, p 18)

True dialogue in RE can be exhausting. However, it can create a space in which pupils can learn how to think. A pupil once said, 'She is a good teacher, she does our thinking for us!' But surely a good teacher does *not* fill the space for inquiry, but rather opens it up. This type of teaching demands that the teacher reconceptualizes what even the youngest pupils are capable of. Teachers need to trust the pupils: trust their abilities to think deeply, and trust their abilities to discuss respectfully.

In order for dialogue in RE to happen, the pupils need to develop the capacity to listen attentively. Fromm believes that deep listening is something people rarely do because 'they do not take the other person's talk seriously; they do not take their own answers seriously', and 'as a result the talk makes them tired' (Fromm 2013, p 89). Julie, a trainee teacher, wrote, 'I believe by discouraging children's voices in the classroom, we are effectively telling them over and over again that they are not worth listening to, affecting their self-esteem or their learning or both'. She felt passionately about this because she felt she had not had a chance to develop her own skills of listening and speaking in her own primary RE.

> This made me feel belittled and I had to struggle to prevent myself from reacting in ways which would have had a negative effect on my learning. If this experience is shifted to a teacher-child encounter in the classroom I would expect a child's feelings to be no different from my own.

Palmer (2001) refers to listening people into speech, implying a total, patient concentration of the self to others and their well-being. How wonderful it would be if the RE classroom taught pupils these two life skills and they grew to be unafraid of true dialogue for life.

How can pupils develop spiritually, morally, socially and culturally in effective RE?

All schools are expected to help pupils develop spiritually, morally, socially and culturally. These four dimensions (also referred to as 'SMSC') are well established in policy documents – with spirituality first becoming a statutory element of schooling in 1944. If we want to use pupils' ideas in RE, one of the best ways is to start with thinking about pupils as spiritual, moral, social and cultural. All too often, as the introduction to this chapter says, teachers think of pupils as 'blank slates'. This is true of spiritual, moral, social and culture aspects of pupils, just as it is true of other intellectual and personal qualities. One of the reasons that teachers – experienced teachers, as well as new teachers – find this difficult is the problem of definition. On spirituality, Priestley celebrates the very ambiguity of the term:

> The spirit ... is dynamic. The spirit denotes life. The traditional images of the spirit are those of wind, fire, running water and many others. They cannot be arrested without ceasing to be what they are. To freeze the spirit is to kill the organism. ... This is why we surrender the whole argument the moment we fall into the trap of agreeing to define. To define is to put sharp edges round a blurred idea, to arrest motion. It is akin to asking a child on a stormy day to go out into the playground and to collect a jar of wind and to bring it back into the classroom for analysis. There can only be one outcome, namely the assertion 'there is nothing in it'. The wind, the fire, the rushing stream must be felt, they must be assessed by their consequences. One never steps into the same river twice, as the Buddhist saying goes. If education is a process and process is defined by dynamism then we have to acknowledge that static measurements are inevitably limited, with clear implications for inspection, it has to be said.
>
> (Priestley 1997, p 29)

Priestley's description (not definition) of spirituality contains echoes of Aristotle's writing from more than two millennia ago. He describes some theories of the spirit or soul and notes that 'all, then, it may be said, characterize the soul by three marks, Movement, Sensation, Incorporeality' (Aristotle 1984, p 646).

So, Priestley and Aristotle, two of the leading writers on spirituality, leave us with *ambiguous* descriptions of spirituality. Some people think of ambiguity as being vague. We prefer to think of ambiguity as being rich in many meanings, as poetry or art is at its best. And we think spirit or soul is important and worth promoting. There is a large set of people in philosophy and in religion who are 'dualists', who believe there are two distinct types of substance or two dimensions. They are likely to believe that the spirit is a different kind of substance to the material. At one point, Ofsted gave such a description: 'spiritual development is the development of the non-material element of a human being which animates and sustains us and, depending on our point of view, either ends or continues in some form when we die' (Ofsted 2004, p 12). More recently, Ofsted has supported a more relational version of spirituality, more like that of Hay (Hay with Nye 2006, Hay 2007). Ofsted's guidance is concerned with pupils' 'ability to be reflective about their own beliefs, religious or otherwise, that inform their perspective on life and their interest in and respect for different people's faiths, feelings and values', their 'sense of enjoyment and fascination in learning about themselves, others and the world around them', their 'use of imagination and creativity in their learning' and their 'willingness to reflect on their experiences' (Ofsted 2016, p 35). This is more like Hay's 'relational consciousness' which he said was 'a biologically inbuilt aspect of our psychology' (Hay 2007, p 14). Hay's best-known work is *The Spirit of the Child* (Hay with Nye 2006), and here, working with Rebecca Nye, he gave examples of how pupils talked about their 'awareness-sensing', 'mystery-sensing' and 'value-sensing' – all described as examples of spiritual experiences.

You may believe that spirituality is mostly about the 'immaterial' aspects of life and inward-looking reflection, or mostly about the 'relational' aspects of life (relationship with the self, but also with other people, the rest of the world and for many also the sacred and divine). Whichever you believe, when teaching RE, you can give pupils opportunities to think about and experience spirituality. RE is not the only subject that should help with spiritual development (*every* subject should be involved), but it would be very odd if pupils went through RE without ever thinking about spiritual issues. Have you given pupils opportunities to think deeply about issues? Have you helped them reflect on their beliefs, and have you helped them think about other people's beliefs? Have they thought about their relationships with the world (with the environment, as well as with other people), and have they been able to think about what it would mean to be in touch with the sacred and divine? This is not a simple matter, and it means trusting the pupils. You cannot 'instruct' pupils to be spiritual. The comedian Billy Connolly used to describe his 'music appreciation' lessons, when the teacher would put some music on and shout at the pupils 'Appreciate! Appreciate!' That doesn't work well for music appreciation, and it won't work any better for spiritual development. Have confidence, as spirituality is – according to just about everyone who ever studied it – part of what it means to be human. Pupils find it easier than adults to experience the awe and wonder that characterizes much that is called spiritual, and they certainly spend a lot of time thinking about deep issues, matters of life and death. The art of the teacher is to allow some of that to be explored in lessons. As Stone says, spiritual development requires 'opportunities to reflect on experience, to explore feelings as well as ideas, to develop the imagination as well as the memory', and this means that we 'engage the whole of a child's being in the process of education' so they 'become important in their own right' (Stone 1995, p 5). Spiritual development may also involve solitude and the desire for the silence of nature – we speak without voice to the trees and the clouds and the waves of the sea – the solitude of listening to poetry, reading it, listening to music or viewing works of art. At such times, we are alone even in the midst of crowds, but we are not lonely, as described by Moustakas and Moustakas (2004, p 142).

Here are some pictures and texts created by pupils, to explain spirituality.

My spirit picture represents a free spirit in its own world where it feels free to be happy and do what it wants. The main point is that any spirit, human or animal should and is entitled to have its own space and freedom. Thinking before I produced this picture I wanted to make it vibrant and to stand out, hopefully full of life. What I'm proud of in the picture is that you can see and feel the energy flowing through the artwork. (Figure 6.5)

Figure 6.5 Spirit picture, by Hannah (aged eleven)

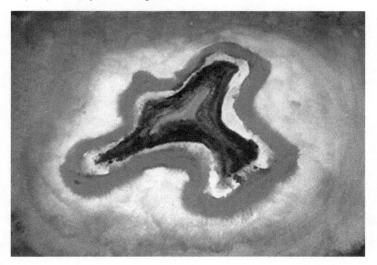

My picture is about travelling the world and finding new destination's all around the world. Also finding your veary own destination, and once you find it God will find you. Traveling the world is like traveling your life and adding new things to it. Going on a spiritual journey will bring out your inner life and loving the earth will give you more things to love and enjoy. (Figure 6.6)

The spiritual can be nurtured through pupils raising and exploring questions of meaning and purpose. It can be nurtured by reflection and developed through opportunities for awe and wonder. Picture this – a teacher sits on the floor surrounded by a group of pupils held spellbound. The teacher is holding a small brown case something akin to a walnut in their hand. As the pupils watch, a small creature emerges – rests for a while and then as its wings dry out, takes off and flies around the pupils and off into the distance. A magical moment – full of awe, wonder and spirituality. Why?

Figure 6.6 Spiritual journey, by Ellie (aged ten)

Task five: A quiet spirituality

Think about all the definitions and descriptions of spirituality that you can find in this chapter and beyond. Find out from the pupils you teach, how they understand different aspects of spirituality. This will help you understand your own position, and it will, we hope, also encourage you to trust that pupils have their own beliefs – which may be different to your beliefs, and different to the beliefs of other pupils.

- Start a session inviting your pupils to join with you in a period of silence. The first time you do this, it may last just thirty seconds. If you try it once or twice a week over several weeks, you will be able to extend the silence to perhaps two or three minutes. Do not tell them what to think in that time. At the end of the silent time, invite the pupils to draw or write what they were thinking about during the silence. (It may be that they thought of nothing: there is no 'correct' way to experience silence!) If they are willing to share with you what they thought about, this can be an interesting experience for you. (It is probably best not to do this as a whole-class discussion, as the pupils may have been thinking about very personal things.) Research by Ng (2012) found that in these circumstances, pupils thought about many, varied things – and it was certainly possible to find spirituality in all its guises, in the pupils' drawings and writing.

You may find the books *Don't Just Do Something – Sit There* and *'See' RE* (Stone 1995, Stone and Brennan 2009) useful for developing stilling exercises with the pupils.

Such simple exercises can transform your views of the pupils you teach. Here is one of the drawings from Ng's research (Figure 6.7):

Figure 6.7 Why am I always the one?, by Bertha (aged seven to eight, reproduced by permission of Yee-Ling Ng)

This can tell us about the child's relationships with others – and with herself.

As well as spirituality, you can help develop pupils morally, socially and culturally in RE lessons. These three terms are complex, but there is not as much controversy over the meaning of the terms as there is with spirituality. Ofsted described them helpfully in these ways:

> Moral development is about the building, by pupils, of a framework of moral values which regulates their personal behaviour. It is also about the development of pupils' understanding of society's shared and agreed values. It is about understanding that there are issues where there is disagreement and it is also about understanding that society's values change. Moral development is about gaining an understanding of the range of views and the reasons for the range. It is also about developing an opinion about the different views.
>
> (Ofsted 2004, p 15)

Social development is about young people working effectively with each other and participating successfully in the community as a whole. It is about the development of the skills and personal qualities necessary for living and working together. It is about functioning effectively in a multi-racial, multi-cultural society. It involves growth in knowledge and understanding of society in all its aspects. This includes understanding people as well as understanding society's institutions, structures and characteristics, economic and political principles and organisations, roles and responsibilities and life as a citizen, parent or worker in a community. It also involves the development of the inter-personal skills necessary for successful relationships.

(Ofsted 2004, p 19)

Cultural development is about pupils' understanding their own culture and other cultures in their town, region and in the country as a whole. It is about understanding cultures represented in Europe and elsewhere in the world. It is about understanding and feeling comfortable in a variety of cultures and being able to operate in the emerging world culture of shared experiences provided by television, travel and the internet. It is about understanding that cultures are always changing and coping with change. Promoting pupils' cultural development is intimately linked with schools' attempts to value cultural diversity and prevent racism.

(Ofsted 2004, p 23)

We can go straight from these definitions to exploring with the pupils you teach how they can learn morally, socially and culturally. RE provides a wealth of opportunities to do this, as it draws on the whole of the world's cultures, societies and moral systems.

Task six: The moral, social and cultural

The moral can be developed through thinking about moral issues raised in everyday life and in RE how religions and worldviews consider solutions. These might be encountered through story and asking the pupils what they think should happen at various points and the implications for all when right choices are not made.

- Choose two stories, one from each of two religious traditions. (Choose stories that the pupils do not already know.) At key 'decisive' points in the story, stop and ask the pupils to think about what the character should do, and why. Ask them to agree, in small groups, what the character should do. Asking pupils to agree on a moral position is important: it gives them a chance to defend their views, and to be flexible enough to change their views, in the light of arguments from other pupils. (You could instead use a 'conscience alley' technique borrowed from drama teachers, as described at https://dramaresource.com/conscience-alley/)

The pupils may develop socially through effective RE by meeting those who hold different beliefs and faith communities. Practical RE such as visiting places of worship can help the pupils engage, as can inviting visitors in to school. Pupils, through schooling and especially in RE (where pupils engage with people and practices from all around the world), learn how to live with each other.

- Choose two significant people from different religious traditions. Choose people who have some challenges in their lives. (It may be best to avoid the holiest of figures, to reduce the possibility of causing offence.) After studying the people, ask the pupils to compose a letter to and from an 'agony aunt'.

    The character's letter might begin 'Dear …, I am having a lot of troubles: no one seems to like me, and following my religion has caused so many problems, such as …'.

    The agony aunt's letter might begin 'Dear …, This is what I would recommend …'.

Working on the troubles of an important religious person can help pupils understand or even overcome some of their own worries. And the social skills developed, in understanding the problems, and in recommending solutions to the problems, will be valuable to your pupils.

Cultural development can be enhanced through engagement with various forms of art and expression, considering how something may be thought beautiful by one person whereas another would find it aesthetically challenging.

- Choose one work of art, and one piece of music, from different religious traditions. The internet now provides ample opportunities to access art and music from every religious and non-religious tradition you can imagine: you can use images.google.com to search 'hindu art' or YouTube to search 'muslim music', or you can use specialist religious sites for individual religions: either way, you should check that the art/music is an appropriate representation of the religion. Ask the pupils to answer these questions about each item:

    What do you think the artist/musician is trying to tell, in this work of art or piece of music?

    What have you learned about the religious tradition, from this work of art or piece of music?

Cultural awareness is enhanced by understanding a 'piece of culture' both from the perspective of the producer and from your own perspective. That is the basis of the two questions to be asked. The viewpoint – or 'horizon' – of the producer, and the viewpoint – or horizon – of the viewer/listener may, with practice, overlap more and more. RE has the massive advantage over other subjects – even English (which is largely limited to written texts, and texts in the English language) – in drawing on a massive global history of rich and varied cultures.

Summary

This chapter has explored the various ideas that pupils bring to RE, and how we can find out about them. The skill of listening to pupils is important to every moment of schooling, but it is especially important when it comes to pupils' ideas on the important 'life and death' issues covered by RE. The subject includes plenty of disagreements and conflicts, and handling such differences makes for wonderful social and moral education. It should also be spiritually developing and – given the sources of religions and non-religious worldviews from around the world and throughout history – it is certainly culturally valuable too. Curiosity can drive teachers, and curious teachers will make for curious pupils – pupils who will want to continue learning, long after they have left our classrooms.

Recommended reading

Alexander, R J (ed) (2010) *Children, Their World, Their Education: Final Report and Recommendations of the Cambridge Primary Review*; Abingdon, Oxfordshire: Routledge.

Stern, L J and Shillitoe, R (2018) *Evaluation of Prayer Spaces in Schools: The Contribution of Prayer Spaces to Spiritual Development*; York: York St John University (also available online at https://ray.yorksj.ac.uk/id/eprint/3103/ and https://www.prayerspacesinschools.com/research2017).

Chapter 7
Assessing Children in Religious Education

Chapter objectives

- Assessing and valuing pupils and their work in RE
- What does good practice in assessment look like in RE?
- The assessable and the unassessable in RE
- Using assessment to promote and report on pupils' learning in RE

Introduction

Assessment is a worrisome thing for teachers. New teachers worry about getting it right, experienced teachers worry about the amount of time it takes, and teachers at every stage worry that someone above them in the hierarchy will judge them according to their quality as assessors. Pupils worry, too. Worry that they are not good enough, if they are assessed negatively; worry that they cannot keep being so good, if they are assessed positively. Pupils take assessment personally. So do adults. All of this worry needs to be tackled head-on. This chapter starts with an account of assessment that draws together some of the basic principles of assessment with related principles and practices in religious and non-religious traditions. Moving on to good practice in RE assessment, there is a consideration what can and, importantly, what cannot – or should not – be assessed in RE. The importance of assessment as a way of promoting learning is central to the whole chapter, but there is also consideration of 'accountability' in RE assessment: ways in which teachers are held accountable to senior staff, to parents and to others outside the school for their assessment work. There are some problems with assessment that will never go away, and these – and responses (if not solutions) to them – are scattered throughout the chapter.

Assessing and valuing pupils and their work in RE

So, what is assessment? All assessment involves making a judgement or determining a value of someone or something. That should already remind you of religious and non-religious traditions of judgement – including the Day of Judgement or Dooms-day. In Jewish, Christian and Muslim traditions, judgement happens – variously – at the moment of death, or at a date in the future when all are judged. The fearful nature of such judgement is a clue, also, to the fearful experience of more mundane forms of assessment in school. But there are many opportunities for assessment in life, and in school, and all are ways of expressing what you value in the pupils you teach and in the work that they do. If you cannot find value in your pupils or in their work, look harder. Assessment processes can help you do this. Forms of assessment used in school include the following:

- Criterion-referenced assessment. This involves assessing according to an independent set of criteria. (A '4' might mean the work is of a particular level, such as meeting the criteria for 'level 4' on some independent scale.) Think of lists of religious rules, such as the 613 mitzvot in Judaism, the 5 precepts of Buddhism or the 10 commandments of both Judaism and Christianity. These include both positive and negative instructions: things to do (like loving your neighbour), and things to avoid doing (like killing). These are 'criteria' by which you might be judged.

- Norm-referenced assessment. This involves assessing performance according to the performance of other people, whether it is better or worse or the same as the 'norm'. (A '4' might mean the work is among the best of the pupil's particular year group.) Both religious and non-religious traditions have 'models' of behaviour, and pupils are judged by such norms. Being more like Mother Teresa, the Buddha, Guru Gobind Singh or Albert Einstein, and being judged in terms of how they lived their lives: this is norm-referenced assessment.

- Summative assessment. This involves assessing the value of a whole set of work or study, at the end of a period of work. (A '4' might be the number printed on a certificate.) Most versions of the Day of Judgement are summative – taking into account your whole life – and are therefore examples of summative assessment.

- Formative assessment. This involves assessing something so as to influence the next period of learning. (A '4' might mean you'll need to do some more revision if you are going to do well in the end of year test.) In Hindu traditions, *karma* describes how good intentions and good deeds lead to greater happiness, while bad intentions and bad deeds lessen future happiness. This may also affect future lives, in the cycle of reincarnation. It could be described as an eternal system of formative assessment.

- Ipsative assessment. This involves assessing a person or a person's work according to that person's previous performance: is it getting better, worse or just the same. (A '4' might mean you have improved a lot since the last assessment.) Various forms of redemption from sin or atonement for sins – in many religions – describe ways in which people are judged not simply for what they have done, but for how they have 'improved' (or been improved) in their lives.

These examples are helpful reminders that assessment is not something restricted to schools, and is certainly not restricted to tests, exams and other kinds of formal assessments. School assessment may be used to judge a *child*, or to judge a child's *work*. It may be also used to judge you as a teacher (as a person), and to judge your teaching and its effectiveness. Increasingly, assessment is used to judge whole schools (to put them into league tables), groups of schools (to inform policy) or national education systems (with the leaders of each country boasting of, or ashamed of, their position in international league tables).

But let us keep this simple, for now. The everyday assessment that fills so much of teachers' lives consists especially of marking. The rest of this chapter will look more at the 'judgement' itself (the mark, grade, level or other consequence of the assessment), but this section ends with an analysis of written comments that you will put on pupils' work. Making written comments on pupils' work is time-consuming – it often takes up some lesson time, and quite a lot of lunchtime and after-school time and evenings and weekends. It is a chore. But – without wanting to sound too much like Mary Poppins – even chores can be made interesting. And various pieces of research suggest that the written feedback comments you will provide for your pupils are some of the most personal and influential communications you will have with them. Among pupils (aged nine to ten years) in the 'spirit of assessment' research, who had looked at teacher comments on various pieces of work, one said 'nice comments i am proud of this work'. Another said 'I feel proud of this comment', while another said 'the things that the teacher said makes the child want to improve'. In contrast, some felt 'left out' by comments: 'I thought it was a good piece of work and she [the teacher] hasn't marked anything (both pages)'. One pupil said that the teacher's comments were 'shamed/upsetting', while another said 'the teacher is very harsh and upseting the pupil' (Stern and Backhouse 2011, p 341). 'All she has done', said one pupil, 'is marked mastakes agine!!!', while another said that 'Pointing out moor spellings mastakes makes me feel very bad inside' (Stern and Backhouse, 2011, p 342). 'Please say why you like it!' was the rather sad comment from another pupil (Stern and Backhouse 2011, p 343).

Task one: The spirit of assessment

The 'spirit of assessment' research looked for any evidence in written assessment feedback of mentions of other people (e.g. 'that's good, and you could have mentioned the story of Rama and Sita too'), comments that suggest you are treating the pupil like a real person (e.g. 'you should feel proud of this work, Yana'), comments that indicate you are being magnanimous (e.g. 'wow – I hadn't thought of that myself!'), comments that might help friendship thrive (e.g. 'it is good to know you've talked to other people about this'), comments that are part of a dialogue (e.g. 'that's interesting – and it would be great if you could tell me more about what happens next') and comments that help the pupil be more creative (e.g. 'what's best about this is that you've put together ideas from two religions – why not try some more?'). Look out for all these qualities, in your own written assessment feedback.

- Look at a set of RE work that has been marked – if possible, marked by you. Write down all the 'writing' by the teacher. That means every tick (if ticks are used), every comment, every mark. Find examples of some of the qualities described above (about people, magnanimity, creativity and so on), and find examples of the opposite (comments that isolate the pupil, that are unfriendly, that stop further dialogue and so on).

- Now, get your pupils to work in groups of two or three to look at some examples of marked work. (You can copy a piece of marked work – this time, including the work as well as the comments.) Ask them to agree on how they feel about having their work marked in this way, perhaps starting with a simple word association game of 'what comes to mind, when you hear the word "marking"?'

- Then, ask the pupils to agree, in those same groups, about what they think marking *should be like*.

- Then, ask the pupils to agree, in those same groups, about what they think marking *should not be like*.

If you complete Task One, you'll have a good idea of what you think, yourself and about assessment feedback, and you'll have a good idea of what pupils think about it, too. This will help you develop good practice in assessment in RE.

What does good practice in assessment look like in RE?

Good practice in RE assessment is a mixture of practice that would be good in any subject, and some qualities that are specific to RE. Over the years, there have been moves to have more criterion-referenced assessment, more normative assessment, more ipsative assessment, more formative assessment and so on. For more than twenty years, UK primary schools focused on levels which were criterion-referenced – the levels work up through a set of numbers, and were integrated from early years through to higher education. More recently, there has been a move 'beyond levels', trying to look more at how all pupils succeed (or not) within their own year group and key stage; that is, assessment has become more normative. Good practice in assessment is partly about knowing what systems each school uses, and if it is using them accurately. But it is more than this. Good RE assessment will also help build your relationships with the pupils, it will contribute to their developing understanding of religious and non-religious ways of life, it will be fair and it will be timely.

First, good practice in RE assessment includes following the guidance provided by the school. This is not simply about being obedient. Schools set up assessment processes and policies in order to help assessment to make sense to everyone in the school – to the pupils, of course, as well as to other teachers and professionals in the school, and to families. Understanding the school system and applying it to RE is a good start, and trying to get to understand the system will also help you explain the system to your own pupils. (They may have forgotten what 'sp' means, what a 'target' is or why some comments are in one colour and some in another.) Once you are following the school's system, you will be able to talk to your pupils about why they are doing better (or worse) in RE than in history or art or PE or literacy/English, and how they can get (even) better. You will be able to talk sensibly to parents at a parents' evening, explaining what and how their daughter is doing in all subjects – rather than just saying what an 'interesting', 'lively' or 'quiet' pupil she is. Working with the school assessment system means you should be able to have meaningful conversations with pupils, with colleagues and with parents about achievement in RE and every other subject. RE certainly deserves to be talked about as much – and as clearly – as any other subject.

CASE STUDY: Shabbat

The Year 2 pupils have been thinking about special days in the Jewish, Christian and Muslim traditions. They have spent the first two lessons learning about Jewish Shabbat traditions, and have learned about

- Shabbat as a day of rest, derived from the account of the creation;
- what Jews can and cannot do on Shabbat, and the need for rules;
- the Shabbat meal and the roles of different family members;
- the Havdalah ceremony and why this is important.

The teacher decides to assess what the pupils have learned about Shabbat, before turning to two more special days in Islam and Christianity. How would you assess what the pupils understand about the deeper meaning of Shabbat for Jewish people? The learning and the assessment is to take place on 'No pencil Wednesday'. You have a camera and want to use this, and you want to get the pupils to work in groups on collaborative displays. Describe the assessment you would plan, for these circumstances.

For all the systems and policies, assessment will not be really good unless it is also used by you to help develop your relationships with pupils, and their confidence in the subject. We hear too often from parents about their pupils coming home from school crying, or saying they hate a teacher or a subject, as a result of an assessment that is more negative than they expected, unfair or absent. ('Absent' assessment hurts most when a pupil has put a lot of effort into a piece of work, and thinks the work has not been appreciated.) Even a high mark may seem mean, if it is not accompanied by a comment, or if it is accompanied by a negative comment – such as 'why can't you always work like this?' or 'did someone else help you with this?' or 'this is very good – for you'. Whenever you are assessing pupils' work, think about how you can use this opportunity to improve your relationship with them, and to improve their confidence as learners. This is not about being a 'generous' marker – pupils do not have confidence in teachers who give away high marks too easily. It is about trying to understand how the pupil has understood things and how they might understand more. Suppose a pupil has written quite a lot, and it is all wrong. You could give an appropriate mark (according to the school's system) and add a comment. Which of these two comments do you think would do more to improve your relationship with the pupil and help the pupil's confidence?

- This is all wrong. You must do it again. Before doing it again, *read the question*. It doesn't say, 'why do people have a party in the Spring?', it says 'why do *Sikhs celebrate Baisakhi*?'

- You've worked hard on this. I know you understand all about the festival, because you've talked about it in class. Could you have a go at saying why Baisakhi is really important to Sikhs?

Both comments will be understood by the pupil as meaning they have got the answer wrong. The second comment, however, starts by saying something positive that is also true (that they have worked hard), and goes on to express your confidence in the pupil (saying that you know they really understand it), before saying what the topic should be and that the pupil should have another go.

One of the words that should probably be banned from assessment is the word 'but'. In any sentence with the word 'but' in the middle, the first half of the sentence is being denied. A grown-up example: if someone says to you 'I really love you, but ...', you know that the sentence is going to end badly. Saying to a pupil 'you compared Christian and Muslim birth rituals well, but ...' has the same effect on the pupil. It is no good complimenting someone and then saying 'but'. The compliment is thrown away by the 'but'. Instead, just change 'but' into 'and'. So you can say to a pupil 'you compared Christian and Muslim birth rituals well, and ...'. Whatever is in the second half of the sentence, the pupil will feel more positive – and will accept the compliment in the first half of the sentence.

As well as following the school's assessment system, and using assessment as a way of building relationships and confidence, a third aspect of good practice in RE assessment is to make the assessment related to RE itself. Although this may sound obvious, it is surprising how much assessment – in every subject – is 'generic'. The marks or grades are generic and there is no explanation about what a '4' means in RE that is different to a '4' in history or numeracy or science. And the comments are generic too – all too often a series of ticks or crosses and comments such as 'good', 'unfinished', 'spelling' or 'underline'. All of these comments may be useful, but none of them are specific to RE. If most of the comments are about the presentation of the work, and none of them are about the subject itself, then pupils will get the idea that you only care about presentation, and do not care about the subject. So, alongside (or instead of) comments about presentation, or other generic comments, say something about RE. 'You've described the Hajj really well' is better than 'You've described this really well' or 'You've demonstrated high level descriptive skills'. If you keep using RE terminology, and keep talking and writing about RE, when the pupils are studying RE, this will be how they learn the subject. If you only talk and write about their spelling and punctuation and handwriting, then, important as these qualities are, this will be all that the pupils learn – they will not think that learning *RE* is at all important.

CASE STUDY: Hindu deities

As part of their six-week module on Hindu beliefs about god, Year 4 pupils have done the following:

- recognized the different people they are to others, for example, student, brother, friend;
- used this understanding to learn about the different avatars of Brahma;
- learned about the Trimurti and researched stories about them;
- visited a local mandir and researched Hindu forms of worship;
- considered a Hindu creation story;
- brought all this learning together to consider the impact such belief has for Hindu life and practice.

The teacher, in planning, does not want to leave the assessment to the end of the module, and wants to build in formative as well as summative assessment opportunities throughout the sessions.

How would you do this? How would you ask the pupils to evidence their understanding of the main religious concepts covered in this module?

How might you incorporate art, drama, computing and written work into the assessment of learning?

According to the *Big Ideas for Religious Education* document, pupils will develop in RE through gaining a deeper and/or a wider understanding of the subject. This will include 'increasing the level of detail; moving from local to global contexts; making increasing links between smaller ideas; including exceptions and contrasts; moving from simple to complex and controversial ideas' (Wintersgill 2017, p 16). The document goes on to describe what younger and older pupils might expect to be able to understand. Just using the phrases, though, will help make your assessment feedback more helpful to the pupils. For example, 'you've got a lot of useful detail on marriage ceremonies', or 'I'd like to hear some more detail about marriage ceremonies', is more helpful and a more RE-specific comment than 'Well done' or 'More needed'.

Fairness is the fourth quality to be highlighted here. From a very early age – well before they get to school – pupils develop a strong sense of what is fair and what is unfair. Fairness is really the junior version of justice, and it is important that pupils keep hold of their sense of fairness and develop it in later life into a concern for justice – not just for themselves, but for everyone. Good practice in RE assessment means being fair – being just. It is painful for teachers to realize this, but even the most experienced teachers who pride themselves on how fair they are will bring some pre-judgements into the assessment process. ('Prejudice' is a more loaded version of 'pre-judgement'; they both mean the same.) A confession. Many teachers (ourselves included) have sat at home, marking work, and have found themselves writing a mark and comments on a piece of work, having assumed it is by one pupil. Then they have looked again at the front of the book, and seen it is by another pupil, and have said to themselves 'Oh, I don't think it deserves that mark if it's by *her*'. It is an embarrassing moment. Any teacher might be less generous in their marking of work by a pupil who misbehaves a lot, or who doesn't seem to like the teacher or the subject; any teacher might be more generous in their marking of work by a pupil who is enthusiastic and well behaved in class. It may be hard to overcome these pre-judgements altogether, but it is important to keep trying. Being fair means marking the work as it is, not according to what you think of the pupil who produced the work. Very few teachers will realize they assess according to what they think of the *pupil*, rather than marking the pupil's *work*. But years of research evidence, as well as our own experience, supports this idea. Ways of avoiding such unconscious unfairness include assessing work as anonymously as you can (e.g. not reading the name before you start assessing work), checking one or two pieces of assessed work (including one by a pupil you don't get on with) with another teacher and – now and again – imagining that *every* piece of work is by your favourite pupil.

Pupils often know how fair or unfair you are in your assessments. They will not always tell you, of course. Benjamin (2002) talked with secondary-age pupils, who all realized that teachers had three ways of talking (and writing) about achievement. There was a discourse of 'normal success', which teachers used with the majority of pupils. Secondly, there was also a discourse of what she called 'really disabled success', which was used by teachers to talk about the achievements of pupils with very significant special educational needs or disabilities. The third type of achievement talk, noticed by the pupils, was the most interesting. It was the discourse of 'consolation success'. This was used with pupils who were not achieving so well, but were not identified as having special needs. Typical 'consolation' assessment talk was 'that's very good – for you', or giving someone a smiley sticker for having completed a piece of work, however badly, because the pupil normally left things unfinished. 'Consolation' success is like a pat on the head, and it does not feel good to pupils. (It is like the 'learned helplessness' described by Dweck 2006.) A pupil aged seven in another piece of research (Hatfield 2004) was reluctant to respond to the question 'describe the three most recent or memorable times the school made you feel good about yourself'. After quite a lot of encouragement, he finally said 'the first day I was at school' – three years ago. 'Why?', the researcher asked. 'Because I thought I could learn.' That pupil had gone home every day with smiley stickers and 'well done!' written in his books. But for three years, he had not believed that his teachers really thought he was doing well. He understood all their 'praise' as merely 'consolation' – as 'very good – for you'. Fairness in assessment means finding out what pupils can do, and helping them build on that. It should not mean patting them on the head while giving them the impression that they cannot ever actually learn much.

Finally, good practice in RE assessment is timely practice. Starting with an adult example, if you ask someone 'do you like my new haircut?', then it makes a difference whether your friend says 'yes, it's wonderful' straight away, or hesitates first, and then says 'yes, it's wonderful'. And you would give up altogether if the friend said 'I'll let you know in a day or two'. Quick positive feedback is better than slow positive feedback. Good practice in assessment means – among other things – *quick* practice. Pupils, even more than adults, will respond well to quick (and fair, and relevant) feedback. If they have to wait for feedback, they will probably ignore the feedback when it comes, and will certainly not associate it with the work itself. It will simply be part of the 'background noise' of the classroom. Many teachers will say that they would love to do their assessments quickly, but they are so busy and there is such a lot of assessment to do, they cannot do this. A secret: if you are going to complete assessments, whether you do them on the same day as the pupils do the work, or a week later, it will take the same amount of time. So it is worth assessing and handing back work quickly – and spending no more time on it than if you assess it and hand it back slowly. You will have done no more (or less) hard work, but the impact of your assessment on pupil learning and confidence will be much greater.

Task two: Have we been on the whole?

A teacher used to tell pupils at the end of every day how they had behaved and how they had learned. 'Today you started off a bit restless, but later on you did some really good science work, and on the whole you were good', he might say. Every day, he presented a summary of behaviour and learning, followed by an 'on the whole you were …' comment. One day, he described the behaviour and the learning, and stopped there. 'But sir', one of the pupils called out, 'were we on the whole?'

I tell that story because, whatever teachers think they are doing when they are assessing, it is most important to understand how the *pupils* understand the assessment. The best way to help pupils understand assessment, and to find out whether they understand assessment, is to make them into assessors.

- For a series of RE lessons or a significant RE project (such as a visit to a place of worship along with the preparation and follow-up work), explain to the pupils that they will assess each other's work and provide feedback. Explain that you will also check the assessment to see that you agree with it.

- Preparing for the assessment, explain the school's assessment system, and explain your own approach to assessment – following the school's system, helping build relationships, contributing to the understanding of religious and non-religious ways of life, being fair and timely.

- Look at the pupils' assessment. Mostly, when teachers try this, they are surprised at how careful, accurate, fair and tough pupils are when completing assessment. Give feedback to the pupils on their assessment and feedback work.

The assessable and the unassessable in RE

Assessing RE brings up another important issue. Are there elements of RE that cannot or should not be assessed? There are hundreds of guides to RE, and hundreds of official syllabuses, and in each school, you should follow the appropriate syllabus. Here, an example is given from the *Big Ideas for Religious Education* document, which illustrates well some of the typical aims, purposes and goals described in many of the agreed syllabuses. Read this description carefully:

School aims

Schools should, through their RE programmes, aim systematically to prepare students for the spiritual and intellectual challenges of living in a world with diverse religions and beliefs as well as non-belief.

Purpose

The main purposes of RE should be to enable students to

- understand the ideas, practices and contemporary manifestations of a diversity of religions and non-religious worldviews;
- understand how religions and beliefs are inextricably woven into, and influenced by, all dimensions of human experience;
- engage with questions raised about religions and beliefs, including questions about meaning and purpose in life, beliefs about God, ultimate reality, issues of right and wrong and what it means to be human;
- understand some of the main approaches to the study of religions;
- develop their own beliefs, ideas, practices, values and identities;
- develop the motivation, understanding and skills to make enquiring into religious questions a lifetime activity;
- flourish as responsible citizens of changing local, national and world communities with diverse religions and beliefs.

Goals

RE should aim to develop in students the ability to

- use terms such as 'religion', 'religious', 'non-religious' and 'secular' appropriately whilst understanding their contested nature;
- develop knowledge and understanding of a range of religions and beliefs;
- discern and analyse connections between religions and beliefs and social, economic, political and cultural life;

- make informed comments about religious issues and about the religious dimensions of personal, social, political and cultural issues;

- understand the rationale and consequences of some of the main approaches to the study of religions and non-religious worldviews;

- articulate clearly and coherently their personal beliefs, ideas, values and experiences while respecting the right of others to differ;

- carry out enquiries into the world of religions and beliefs;

- reflect, communicate and act in an informed, intelligent and sensitive manner towards those who profess religions and beliefs and also towards those with no expressed beliefs.

(Wintersgill 2017, p 5)

The 'aims' section is for the school as a whole, and if you are assessing the pupils, you will not be using this description. It may be worth thinking about whether you could assess the school, according to these aims, but that would be difficult – unless you had twenty or thirty years to spare, to see how the pupils grew up to live in the diverse world full of challenges. (This does not mean the 'aims' are unimportant: they are, in fact, likely to be what makes you feel your career is worthwhile, as you see your former pupils grow into mature and responsible adults.) What about the 'purpose' section? Some of these elements may be assessable, such as understanding ideas and practices, and engaging with important questions. Others are not so easily assessable, such as developing their own beliefs, ideas, practices, values and identities – in part, because those take place over such a long period, and in part because the wording suggests an 'ipsative' form of assessment (how have the pupils changed?), which might disadvantage those pupils who come in to your class with clear beliefs, values and identities, and who maintain those beliefs, values and identities. (Is it right to disadvantage pupils who maintain their beliefs, rather than change them?) And the final point – to flourish as responsible citizens – is another long-term item that is impossible to assess within a school (important, but not assessable within the school). However, as with the 'aims' section, these qualities may be used to assess RE in the long term.

It is the 'goals' section that provides more guidance for assessing pupils – and it is, after all, written in the form of developing the abilities of the pupils, rather than the subject or the school. Of the eight goals in the list, some are oriented towards knowledge – using correct terms, developing knowledge. These are relatively easy to assess. Sometimes, teachers think that knowledge is the only quality that should be assessed in primary RE, and they stop there. In the United States, where levels of religious observance are very high, but knowledge of religions is very low, there has recently been a movement to improve 'religious literacy' which, for most advocates, means knowledge of religions. Prothero makes this explicit, saying 'I focus on spreading knowledge rather than inculcating virtues'

(Prothero 2007, p 21). Many pupils think that gaining knowledge is the most important quality to demonstrate – and quick quizzes, in school and on the internet and television, emphasize that dimension of assessment. However, RE in the UK has always had goals that are broader than just knowledge. In the list of bullet points, there are various qualities of 'arguing' or 'debating': making informed comments, articulating personal beliefs, ideas and values, and reflecting and communicating in an informed way. These are harder to assess. You will certainly have to go beyond simple quizzes, and create opportunities for assessing discussions and debates, presentations and/or extended written projects. This is challenging and important. It gets closer to the heart of why RE should be studied, and includes the assessment of qualities that are interpersonal – pupils should be given opportunities to defend their own positions, and treat with respect the different positions of other pupils.

There is a third group of qualities in the 'goals' list, which refer to the qualities of pupils as investigators – as researchers, if you like. Expecting pupils to understand the consequences of how to study the subject and to carry out enquiries: these are qualities that are also expected of university students in their research projects, so it is encouraging to see them listed in goals of school-based RE even in primary schools. Studying religion is challenging – as the religions themselves incorporate different views on and approaches to sources of knowledge and belief. So making pupils into researchers is challenging – and very much worth doing. Books like those of Stern (2006, 2018a) and Freathy (Freathy et al. 2015) recommend seeing primary as well as secondary pupils (and teachers) as researchers in RE lessons. This approach is helpful in overcoming some of the hardest problems in RE, as it uses a range of methods of studying the subject (some more personal and subjective, some more 'scientific' and objective), and leaves the pupils more able to make their own minds up – not only about the topics being studied, but the ways of studying them. Assessing the pupils as researchers is easier than might be thought: pupils can be set investigative work (as suggested in Chapter 5), and be assessed in the same way as university researchers are assessed: how well (how carefully, with how much detail) did they investigate, how original were they, and how well did they share their findings? (University students and staff may be working at a higher level, but they are still assessed by those three criteria.)

Task three: Ask God?

Here is some work from a pupil, aged nine, who was invited to suggest questions to ask 'the one who knows everything' or 'God'. She suggested seven questions, some about creation, one about divine power, one about divine benevolence and some about good and evil. Can the pupil raise a range of important religious questions of her own, based on her understanding of the concept of God? Write some appropriate feedback for this piece of work (Figure 7.1).

Figure 7.1 Ask God? (from Lat Blaylock http://www.natre.org.uk)

There is one word in the 'goals' section that many teachers find difficult to assess. It is the word 'act' in the final bullet. Are teachers supposed to be assessing how pupils behave, as part of their RE assessment? The same question is said of ethics and values education, of citizenship education and of personal and social education. All these subjects – all the 'E' subjects on the curriculum (RE, PSHE, CE – and PE too) – are expected to have some personal impact on pupils; they are expected to learn *from* the topics as well as learn *about* the topics. In RE syllabuses, this is sometimes described as 'learning from religion' and 'learning about religions'. Should this personal impact be assessed? It seems reasonable to assess some of the personal impact. So, in the bullet points above, pupils are expected to 'act in an informed, intelligent and sensitive manner towards those who profess religions and beliefs and also towards those with no expressed beliefs'. This can be assessed in RE lessons, in discussions and debates, in presentations and in role-playing. But if you heard a pupil being religiously disrespectful in the playground, would you include this in your assessment of their RE? Certainly, you might address the issue with the pupil – explain to them that this is not a good way to behave, and remind them of the work they have completed in RE. But it might be less reasonable to include such non-RE-lesson behaviour in an RE assessment.

Such issues sit on the boundary of what should and should not be assessed in RE. There are some things that should definitely not be assessed in RE. These include how religiously devout pupils are, which religion or non-religious way of life they follow and whether or not they agree or disagree with the teacher's views on particular sensitive issues. Although schools are expected to promote 'fundamental British values', this does not mean that any teacher can assess pupils according to whether they agree with their teacher. And whether or not you think that being religious is valuable, you should not be assessing pupils as to whether they are or are not religious. Few teachers would intentionally mark a pupil down if they followed a different religion to that of the teacher (or the rest of the class), but this can happen inadvertently. For example, if all the examples are from one religion, and all the assessment is about one religion, then a pupil from another religion, or from no religion, might be – or might feel – excluded, and might end up doing less well. This can, strangely, work in the opposite way to what might be expected. Some actively religious pupils feel *excluded* in RE lessons. Sometimes this is because they feel that their own religion is being misrepresented, and sometimes this is because other pupils use RE lessons as opportunities to pick on or bully religious pupils. A little religious knowledge can be a dangerous thing: Christian pupils may be picked on for believing in a non-evolutionary creation account, Sikh pupils may be picked on for carrying a small knife round their neck, Buddhist pupils may be picked on because their beliefs are assumed to be pacifist. Whether these are correct or incorrect, for these pupils, RE may bring up difficulties that lead pupils to perform less well in the subject – perhaps simply to 'fit in' with what the teacher or other pupils seem to believe. Liedgren (2018) describes Jehovah's Witness pupils and adults in Swedish schools. They appreciated the teachers who gave them a chance to express their views, and didn't mark them down for expressing them. They also appreciated teachers who read the pamphlets they were given (by the pupil or their parents) even if they disagreed with them, rather than the teachers who pretended to be interested but clearly just put the pamphlets in the bin. These examples suggest that there were teachers who did indeed mark these pupils down for their beliefs, and who treated their views condescendingly.

Most – but not all – aspects of RE can and should be able to be assessed. A final point to make in this section is that there will be times when pupils will not be able to do well in RE. RE deals with personal issues – families, marriage, birth ceremonies, festivals and so on – that are also 'lived' by pupils. A pupil whose family is going through an unpleasant divorce may not feel good about a project on marriage; a pupil who has a miserable Christmas every year because of visits from abusive relatives may perform less well in festive projects; a pupil who is a refugee from a war zone as a result of the rest of the family being executed might find the Easter narrative or the Martyrdom of Guru Arjan too much to cope with. These are examples of the stubborn problems of assessment in RE: problems that should not be ignored or swept under the carpet.

Task four: Lost for words

This is almost an assessment task, a task that sits at the edge of the assessable and the unassessable in RE. The educational psychologist John Holland specializes in supporting schools in dealing with bereavement. In any primary school, some of the pupils will lose a close relative, and teachers often say they are 'lost for words' (Holland 1997, 2016). Difficult aspects of life – such as this, and the breakdown of families, and war – may all be covered in RE lessons. That does not mean that the RE coordinator should be responsible for dealing with all such challenges. Yet RE lessons are places where it might be appropriate to support pupils – all the pupils, not just those who have been through difficult times – in dealing with the problems. What do you say, when, typically, words might fail you? Here is a task to complete as a teacher with other teachers, and as a teacher with pupils in an RE lesson.

- Choose a difficult issue that has come up in your school that might leave you (and others) 'lost for words', such as the death of a pupil's parent.

- Work with pupils (or perhaps with other teachers), on what you might say, when you feel lost for words. John Holland is often asked this question by teachers who say they just do not know what to say. He usually asks them 'well, how do you feel?', and they generally say 'I just feel so sorry for the child'. He might then suggest 'well, why don't you say that?' This is a good start. Try working with pupils to do a role-play of difficult moments in life. The pupils may come up with more ideas of what to say than adults do, as pupils are often less inhibited about such things. However, they rarely get opportunities *within lessons* to show how supportive and sensitive they can be in such situations.

- Follow this up with some work on important moments in the religious or non-religious traditions you are studying. What might be said to a troubled prophet such as Moses (at many moments in his life), to a community that has lost its leader or to a religious group whose temple has been destroyed? You could role-play appropriate conversations. Or you could get older pupils to act like 'agony aunts', and provide written advice to a troubled religious figure.

This approach to dealing with difficult situations is central to the teachings of Buddhism. In that tradition, there are narratives that explain what might be said to a bereaved mother (the story of Kisagotami, for example, at https://www.clear-vision.org/schools/Teachers/teacher-info/Buddhist-stories/Kisa-Gotami.aspx), to an evil murderer or to an impatient pupil (the story of Angulimala and the koan 'what is the sound of one hand clapping', for example, in Chödzin and Kohn 1997, Olson 2005). See Stern 2007, Chapter 8, for worked examples of these with pupils.

If these activities are completed in response to an immediate problem in school, it is probably best not to see them as assessment tasks. But if they are built in to the curriculum, then they can be good ways to assess how pupils reflect, communicate and act in a sensitive manner. You might find that letting others speak for you when your own words fail can be helpful. You can use the words in *Badger's Parting Gifts* (Varley 1984) to explore how to celebrate life and build memories, or those in *Nothing* (Inkpen 1994) to think about regaining identity. Or perhaps the beautiful and haunting story of *The Velveteen Rabbit* (Williams 2007) or *Waterbugs and Dragonflies* (Stickney 1997) that explores death with young children. In Stickney's book, the bugs at the bottom of the pond agree that when their turn comes to climb the lily stalk on their way to the great unknown, they will return to the others to tell them what it is like. The creatures that leave the pond soon discover that being a winged, fragile, free dragonfly, they cannot break through the surface of the water and fly off leaving the others to keep on wondering. Why not google some images and show these while you tell the story with some gentle music playing?

Using assessment to promote and report on pupils' learning in RE

All through this chapter, assessment has been described as an integral part of RE lessons – not as a wholly separate activity completed after the lessons have been finished. This approach emphasizes *formative* assessment, assessment that helps with future performance. Formative assessment can be combined with other approaches to assessment (a test might be 'summative' and also be 'formative', and so on), but it has come into prominence in recent times, often described as 'assessment for learning'. It is a healthy approach as it does not separate out assessment – and it therefore helps avoid the problem of changing pupil motivation. Psychologists talk about 'intrinsic' and 'extrinsic' motivation. In school, a pupil who has an intrinsic motivation to learn RE is learning because they think the learning itself is interesting or enjoyable or worthwhile. A pupil with an extrinsic motivation to learn RE is learning because they think they will get some external reward – a high grade, a certificate, a star on a star chart and perhaps eventually a good place at a university and a well-paid job. Most of us have a mixture of intrinsic and extrinsic motivations – not just as learners, but as teachers too. On a bad day, a teacher will rely on the need for a salary for motivation, on a good day – let us hope, most days – the value of the job itself is the more important motivation. For the pupils, all teachers will provide some extrinsic motivation by having the occasional prizes and rewards for their pupils, but it is important when assessing pupils to give them *intrinsic* motivation. This means your assessments should emphasize the value of learning RE. You can do this by showing an interest in the topic (e.g. simply by saying that you find the pupils' responses interesting), and by talking about how valuable it is to know about how people live their lives and how they answer life's big questions.

Intrinsic motivation is important throughout teaching, but the value of concentrating on it in assessment is that assessment processes too often take over. Learning is completed simply for the sake of the test, or to get higher marks. This will distract pupils from the real value of the subject, and make the subject much 'thinner'. It becomes a means to an end, rather than an end in itself. The best-known advocates of formative assessment, Black and Wiliam (Black and Wiliam 1998, Wiliam 2005), say that if you really want your pupils to get higher grades, you should not tell them what grades they are getting during the year.

When the classroom culture focuses on rewards, 'gold stars', grades, or class ranking, then pupils look for ways to obtain the best marks rather than to improve their learning. One reported consequence is that, when they have any choice, pupils avoid difficult tasks. They also spend time and energy looking for clues to the 'right answer'. Indeed, many become reluctant to ask questions out of a fear of failure. Pupils who encounter difficulties are led to believe that they lack ability, and this belief leads them to attribute their difficulties to a defect in themselves about which they cannot do a great deal. Thus they avoid investing effort in learning that can lead only to disappointment, and they try to build up their self-esteem in other ways.

(Black and Wiliam 1998, p 144)

As a school subject, RE is sometimes looked down upon (unfairly and inaccurately) as less important – less valuable in the job market, less high profile in the league tables. Why not use that stereotype to your advantage and say to the pupils: perhaps RE will not get you the best job in the world, but understanding the meaning of life and how to live well is far more important than doing well in a competition. Your approach to assessment can help with this.

Task five: Growing up

This pupil, aged eight, was asked to imagine taking Bar/Bat Mitzvah as a young Jewish person, and to give 'I feel/because...' sentences that showed what they have learned. Can she describe how Jewish people are accepted as adult members of the community? Can she give simple reasons for a range of feelings experienced in a religious ritual? (See Figure 7.2.)

Figure 7.2 Thoughts of my Bar/Bat Mitzvah (from Lat Blaylock http://www.natre.org.uk)

One way in which assessment can help pupils appreciate their learning is that it can tell them what they have learned. This is such a fundamental aspect of assessment, yet it is often forgotten. A wonderful picture book, *When I Was Born* (Martins and Matoso 2010), describes a child realizing how much they have learned since being born. 'When I was born', it says, 'I had never seen anything. … I didn't know anybody and nobody knew me. … I had never played with stones or got muddy hands. … My feet didn't know how to walk …'. But now, the child sees and does wonderful things:

> Now I know that there is a whole world to discover: millions and millions of things my hands haven't yet reached; millions and millions of lands my feet haven't yet taken me to. And new smells and sounds and tastes. But one thing is certain. Each day I discover something new. And that is the most wonderful thing of all!
>
> Martins and Matoso 2010

The joy of this book is the joy of learning. Pupils can be reminded of this by your assessment work – especially if it is encouraging and builds on what has been done throughout the year. Childhood is a period of intense learning for all pupils – including those who are not regarded as succeeding in school. On average, from the age of four, a child will learn a thousand new words a year until they leave school. That means roughly twenty words a week, or three words a day. (Adults carry on adding to their vocabulary, at a third of the speed – an average of about one word a day.) Very few pupils realize this – and none that I have asked can describe even one or two new words learned in the last week, unless their teachers have a 'new word of the week' (perhaps a 'new RE word of the week'?) on display. Assessment tasks can help pupils realize, and celebrate, the huge amount they are learning.

This idea of assessment as celebration is linked to one of the ways in which you are assessed as a teacher in the school, and how you report to pupils' families about your pupils' progress. At least once every year, you might be asked to report on your pupils' learning in RE to senior staff in the school – perhaps to the RE coordinator (to help with planning RE), to a member of staff reviewing pupil progress or policy on assessment or to a member of staff who is assessing/appraising your own performance. The following task (adapted from Stern 2003 and 2018a) asks you to get your pupils to write about their learning in RE, and it asks members of their families to respond: excellent preparation, then, for a parents' evening, as well as a good way to let others in the school know what is happening in RE. It could be the basis of a celebration for you and your pupils, too.

Task six: We have been studying …

If the head teacher agrees you can do this, then you could ask your pupils to write letters home (to parents or carers) about what they have learned in Religious Education during the year. The first part of the letter could be agreed by the whole class, with the second part individually written by each pupil.

Here is a writing frame:

Dear Parent/Carer

In Religious Education, we have been studying … [the various topics and issues covered in RE, in as much detail as the class can remember]

We enjoy learning about these topics because …

The most important reason for studying these topics, is to know …, to be able to …, and also to understand … and … [explain the various goals of the RE, in terms of knowledge, skills, understanding and personal development]

This will be useful when [or because] …

It would be good to hear about anything you learned in Religious Education when you were in school, or what you have learned since then. You could fill in the slip, below.

To: … Date: …

When I/we did Religious Education in school, and since leaving school at home or at work, my/our favourite topics and activities were/are …

I/we have these ideas or resources that might be useful for Religious Education: …

Name of parent/carer: …

Summary

When assessing RE, it is important to follow the school systems and policies, to help build relationships, to be fair and timely, to address difficult issues with sensitivity (and to know when not to assess) and to be engaging and celebratory. With all this, it is also important to remember that chance will always play a role in assessment. Good luck and bad luck will always have their say. Within Christian traditions, although judgement (the Day of Judgement, or judgement at the end of life) may be based on your religious observance and your actions, there is also a role for God's grace. Grace may lead a greater sinner to go to heaven, while a lesser sinner may not. This does not mean – in any of the theologies I have read – that it is a matter of chance, as the Christian God is all-knowing and so not open to chance. But as far as people go, it may feel like chance, as the 'assessment' you go through (the assessment of your observance and your actions) does not guarantee anything. The same sense of chance is evident in Hindu traditions. In India, a training game called *Moksha Chitram* was developed to teach pupils about life and the possibility of gaining *Moksha* – the ultimate liberation from the cycle of birth and death. The game involved a board, with ladders representing opportunities to gain good *Karma* (actions that would have beneficial consequences), snakes representing bad *Karma* (actions with negative consequences) and *Moksha* represented in the final square. The element of chance in this game was represented by dice, thrown to see on which square you would land. In the nineteenth century, British missionaries saw the game and brought it back to the UK. They made it Christian, by naming the snakes and ladders according to the seven deadly sins and the seven virtues, and calling the game *Snakes and Ladders*. It is still played today, but without any reference to religion. Win or lose, though, chance has its say – and this is a good, if slightly uncomfortable, lesson for assessment in RE too.

Recommended reading

Stern, L J and Backhouse, A (2011) 'Dialogic Feedback for Children and Teachers: Evaluating the "Spirit of Assessment",' *International Journal of Children's Spirituality, 16:*4, pp 331–46.

Wiliam, D (2005) *Formative Assessment: The Research Evidence*; Educational Testing Service (http://www.ets.org/).

Chapter 8
Practical Issues

Chapter objectives

- What is important to consider when planning primary RE?
- How is progress planned into a single RE lesson?
- How is progress planned into a series of RE lessons?
- How can planning address the whole range of pupil abilities and needs?
- How can planning for RE help with planning a career in primary education?
- What is the future of RE?

Introduction

There are so many practical issues faced by primary teachers; it would be easy to feel overwhelmed. For teaching RE, how will the timetable work, what resources and training are available and how should we take account of the views of pupils' families? The focus in this chapter is on giving structure to your work teaching RE. This means thinking about planning – planning the subject and planning your own career. RE is a more changeable subject than most, so teachers are not only planning a 'given' curriculum, they are able to contribute to the development of the subject as a whole. Surprise might be important to education (as described in Chapter 6), but planning is just as important. As an absolute minimum, planning will help you survive. More than this, planning will make a good teacher into a good *educator*, and will make a teacher who is an excellent performer into a teacher whose pupils are excellent learners. Planning makes learning make sense. Think of each lesson or each element of each lesson as a brick. Without planning, at the end of a series of lessons, what you have is a pile of bricks. *With* planning, what you have is a house. That is why practical issues in RE are covered, here, by a chapter on planning.

What is important to consider when planning primary RE?

Every school, every teacher education provider and every commercial publisher of education books will have their own specific model of planning. You will need to use these. So this book will not provide yet another version of the 'perfect' lesson plan or the 'perfect' planning schedule for a year's worth of learning in RE. Instead, what you will get is a guide to the most important aspects of planning that will help you to gain mastery as an RE teacher. This will take you through planning for an individual lesson, planning for a series of lessons, planning for the whole range of pupils and planning your own career. As this is the final chapter of the book, it will not only consider your own future, but the future of RE itself.

In Task Three of Chapter 2 of this book, there was an exercise working through learning objectives for RE lessons. That was a good introduction to some of the important issues in lesson planning, and you may want to look back at what you did then, before continuing with this chapter. Setting out learning objectives is a good professional way of planning lessons, but in practice, planning starts from *nothing*. Most teachers can remember the first time they took responsibility for a whole class of pupils. Often, they describe a moment of silence. The pupils look at you, the teacher, as if to say, 'so, what are we all going to do today?' That moment feels as though it lasts a lifetime, but is usually just a second or two. Either the teacher starts talking, or the pupils look away and start doing their own thing. But, starting from nothing is the character of every lesson. The lesson (not the pupils, not the teacher) is a 'blank slate', a bright new thing with nothing in it – yet.

- There is a story told, called *Stone Soup*. It is a story of how a meal can come from nothing. The story is popular in many countries, and is variously told as a Christian story (about travelling monks), a Jewish story (about a travelling rabbi), a story of soldiers returning from war, a story of beggars, a Canadian story, an African story, a Portuguese story, a German story, a Chinese story – it is a story that seems to fit every religious, national and cultural tradition. Some travellers, anyway, are hungry and poor, and they come to a village. Without any money, they set up a pot in the middle of the village, fill it with water from the stream and light a fire under it. As villagers congregate, they put a stone into the water. 'What are you doing?', one villager asks. A traveller replies, 'making stone soup – it's delicious – but it could do with a bit more flavour'. The villager brings a few carrots and puts them in the pot, for flavour. 'It could do with some more herbs', so another villager puts some herbs in the pot. This goes on, until a wonderful, nourishing soup is bubbling away in the pot. This, the travellers share with the villagers (Figure 8.1).

As a teacher, you come to the lesson with nothing – or with an apparently insignificant lump of rock. (Perhaps that's the lump in your throat, when facing a class for the first time!) The lesson learned from *Stone Soup* is that, with a bit of ingenuity, and by engaging all the villagers – all the pupils in the class – you can make a wonderful nourishing lesson. But it will not work without your ingenuity, and it will not work without the contributions from the pupils. You provide the planning, the pupils make it all worthwhile.

Figure 8.1 Stone Soup (from http://stonesoupadda.net/)

Although you will always plan your *teaching*, some teachers forget to plan the pupils' *learning*. Teaching is hard work, but the only value of that hard work is the learning of the pupils. It is not enough that they sit quietly in the room while you teach. So, when planning, think about learning. 'Learning' is not a list of topics covered. It might include *remembering* the list of topics covered, but that is a modest achievement. It should include learning of knowledge (some facts or ideas), learning how or why things are as they are (some understanding, especially of the key concepts), learning how to do things (skills) and learning attitudes such as empathy, sensitivity, care and curiosity. These CASK elements (i.e. concepts, attitudes, skills and knowledge) do not need to be treated mechanically – it is not a matter of every lesson including one concept, one attitude and so on. Rather, they provide clues to what it means to learn – rather than what it means to teach. Well, the only judge of teaching is learning, so perhaps they are the same – but teachers, unlike playwrights, are not just planning their own scripts, they are planning for what the pupils will be able to say, too.

In Jewish and Christian accounts of the creation of the world, God spends six days making the world, and on the seventh day contemplates it. This is the origin of the idea of a sabbath, a day of rest. Along with one day a week of rest or contemplation, many religions build in thoughtful rests during each day (e.g. with a rhythm of prayers), and of rests over longer periods (e.g. a jubilee year every fifty years, to help the land rest and recover). If God and the land need to rest, and if people need to rest for religious reasons, why shouldn't teachers rest? A key element in planning – and one that is rarely mentioned in the usual guidance – is to plan thoughtful rest periods into every lesson and every series of lessons. Of course there are rest periods built in to every school day: playtimes and lunchtimes. But teachers all too rarely use these times to rest: they are usually busy supporting the pupils who hang back at the end of the lesson or preparing for the next lesson. During a research project, teachers and pupils were asked how to make the school more of a community. One teacher (in a secondary school) said that he would 'ban all tea and coffee machines' kept in classrooms. This seemed an odd way to make the school more of a community. Asked to explain, he said that this would 'make people come down to one staff room and make everyone sit together' (Stern 2009, p 117). Simply resting and talking together will help teachers.

As well as making good use of playtimes and lunchtimes, teachers should plan for such rest periods in every lesson, too. At some point, will you have engaged the pupils in their own work, in such a way that you can look over the class and see how everyone is doing? Will you be able to deal with an individual pupil who is upset, while the other pupils get on with work you have planned for them? Will you have time, in the middle of the lesson, to rethink what you will be doing later on, if the pupils are getting through the work more quickly (or more slowly) than you had expected? Will you have time to reflect on the lesson, or simply to take a breather and perhaps have a sip of water? If you are planning to be a teacher for a long time, then take a tip from the experienced teachers you see. They are the ones who seem always to have time, and are never – or rarely – flustered in the classroom. They are the ones who have learned the importance of building rest in to every lesson. It is worth repeating what is said earlier: if rest and contemplation are described as being needed by God, surely they are needed by teachers.

Rests are important to plan for the pupils, too. That might include sitting with their heads resting on their arms on the desk, while you tell them a story. It might include times when they think about all they have learned – perhaps just for a minute or so at the end of a school day. One of the most impressive teachers I have seen did not let any pupil leave the classroom until every pupil had described something new they had learned that day – and every pupil had to say a different thing. Once the pupils were used to this, you could see them go into 'contemplation' mode as the lesson or the day was coming to an end, ready for the teacher's question 'so, what did you learn today?' Many educationalists suggest that when you ask a question of the whole class, you should not ask the pupil who is first to put a hand up. You should not ask for hands up, but let the pupils think for a few seconds. Then, you can choose someone – perhaps at random (lolly sticks with pupil names on them in a jar?), or for a particular purpose (perhaps because you've realized that a certain pupil has had an all-too-rare 'lightbulb' moment, and want to celebrate it). Those brief periods of contemplation, of thinking, are valuable. Plan for regular rest and contemplation periods. Pupils and teachers need time to recreate themselves. That is why play and holidays are often called 'recreation' (i.e. re-creation).

Planning primary RE needs to focus on the important ideas in the subject. Every syllabus will have its own description of these ideas. In the *Big Ideas in Religious Education* document, there are six 'big ideas' which are applied to every age group. These relate to continuity and change, how we express ourselves, what a good life is, making sense of life's experiences, community and power, and the 'big picture' (or the 'meaning of life'). In terms of planning, if you ignore this list – or the equivalent lists in the syllabus used in your school – then you are not *planning* RE, you are just planning a set of more-or-less relevant RE activities.

Task one: Build a house

Unplanned RE is just a pile of bricks. Plan a house – a house filled with engaged learners of RE. This is a task for a group of six teachers. Start with a lottery, each pulling a number from one to six out of a hat, with the numbers representing each of the 'big ideas' summarized below (with more detail in Wintersgill 2017 on what they mean for different age groups of pupils).

- Each teacher should plan one activity (a bit of teaching, for the teacher, a bit of learning, for the pupils), taking no more than an hour to research and plan the activity.

- Together, all six teachers should work on how the six separate plans can make sense as a series – in any order – that will help pupils learn more than just the sum of the various parts. Agree on a name – a theme, if you like – for this set of activities.

Big Idea 1: Continuity, Change and Diversity

Religions and non-religious worldviews involve interconnected patterns of beliefs, practices and values. They are also highly diverse and change in response to new situations and challenges. These patterns of diversity and change can be the cause of debate, tension and conflict or result in new, creative developments.

Big Idea 2: Words and Beyond

Many people find it difficult to express their deepest beliefs, feelings, emotions and religious experiences using everyday language. Instead, they may use a variety of different approaches including figurative language and a range of literary genres. In addition, people use non-verbal forms of communication such as art, music, drama and dance that seek to explain or illustrate religious or non-religious ideas or experiences. There are different ways of interpreting both verbal and non-verbal forms of expression, often depending on a person's view of the origin or inspiration behind them. The use of some non-verbal forms of communication is highly controversial within some religious groups, particularly their use in worship or ritual.

Big Idea 3: A Good Life

Many religions and non-religious communities strive to live according to what they understand as a good life. Their members share an understanding as to the sort of characteristics and behaviours a good person will seek to achieve, as well as dealing with what is, or is not, acceptable moral behaviour. People have different ideas about how and why we should lead a good life. The ideal is usually presented in the lives and character of exemplary members. There may be considerable agreement across different religions and non-religious worldviews on some matters, and considerable differences on others. Also, there are often major disagreements over the interpretation and application of moral principles between members of the same religion or worldview.

Big Idea 4: Making Sense of Life's Experiences

Many people have deeply felt experiences, which they may refer to as being religious or spiritual or simply part of what it means to be human. These experiences may result in people undergoing transformative change and on rare occasions the experience of a single person has led to the formation of a new religion or worldview. Through religious rituals and other practices, people sometimes experience a deep connection with God or gods, nature, their own consciousness or with each other. This can give them a heightened sense of awareness and mystery. Many people find that belonging to religious or non-religious groups with others who share their beliefs, values and traditions gives them a sense of identity and belonging.

Big Idea 5: Influence, Community, Culture and Power

Religious and non-religious worldviews interact with wider communities and cultures. They affect the way communities have come to identify themselves over time by shaping their traditions, laws, political systems, festivals, values, rituals and the arts. The patterns of influence vary significantly in different communities and at different points in time. Some communities are influenced predominantly by one religion. More diverse and plural communities are influenced by several religious and non-religious worldviews. Their appeal to a highly respected authority or vision, whether religious or non-religious, can lead them to make positive and life-changing contributions to their communities. It can also give them considerable power, which may lead to both positive and negative outcomes.

Big Idea 6: The Big Picture

Religions and non-religious worldviews provide comprehensive accounts of how and why the world is as it is. These accounts are sometimes called 'grand narratives'. They seek to answer the big questions about the universe and the nature of humanity such as 'Does anything exist beyond the natural world?', 'Is there life beyond death?', 'What is the path to salvation?' and 'Do we have one physical life or many?'. These narratives are usually based on approaches to life, texts or traditions, which are taken to be authoritative. People interpret and understand these traditions in different ways.

(Wintersgill 2017, p 15)

For new teachers, planning is hard work, and the 'nuts and bolts' of planning – the details that go right, and the things that go wrong – are very visible. With experience, planning comes more naturally. It still takes effort but, like driving a car after you have passed your test, it feels and looks much easier. Experienced teachers sometimes look as though they don't plan. Don't be deceived: planning is happening even when you cannot see it. And experienced teachers will even have planned for what happens when they do *not* have a plan. Perhaps a supply teacher already taught the lesson you had planned, or the vital resource – the *murti* – you were going to use to teach the story of Ganesha has disappeared. Have you planned for the moment you have no plan? This is easily done.

- For older pupils, try the alphabet game – write the letters of the alphabet down the side of a piece of paper, and get the pupils (perhaps in groups of two or three) to remember or to find out religious terms beginning with each letter of the alphabet.

- Or find a daily newspaper (a real one, made of paper) and give one page to each group of pupils and get them to discover bits of writing relevant to RE (e.g. births, deaths, festivals, heroes/heroines, people doing good things, people doing bad things, people whose lives have changed).

- Or say you are constructing an RE quiz, and want the pupils to write all the questions: each pupil should think of a good question, and you will collect them all and create a quiz out of them.

These are just three ideas. See if you can think up three more activities. Make sure they are educationally valuable, so that you are not just seeking to 'fill the time'. Once you've planned for the time when you haven't got a plan, you are making planning work for you.

How is progress planned into a single RE lesson?

Think of a single RE lesson. There is a series of five questions that, when answered, create one model of a good lesson plan.

- What do you want the pupils to learn? This is the basis for working out and describing to the pupils the outcomes from the lesson. (Remember that you will plan for the pupils to learn in various ways, but that *other* learning will also take place – unexpectedly – in every lesson, and that will be exciting and surprising.)

- What will you use to get the pupils thinking about the topic? This is the basis for deciding on an object such as a prayer shawl to investigate, a picture such as a *Pietà* of Mary and Jesus to look at, a story to tell such as a heroic tale of Hanuman, the monkey god, or a piece of writing from a sacred text such as the Sikh *Hukamnama* (provided each day at http://www.sikhnet.com/hukam).

- How will you make sure the pupils are understanding this initial stimulus? The pupils might be asked questions, or discuss what they think about, the object, picture, story or writing. This is the stage most often missed by newer teachers – who often go straight from an initial stimulus (an object, a story) to the middle of the lesson, without checking whether the pupils make sense of the stimulus material.

- How will you get them to learn about this topic? This is the core of the lesson, when the pupils are busy doing things, drawing, writing, trying out ideas. The pupils are making sense of the world, with an emphasis on the word 'making'. It is a creative process, learning. Pupils create a new model of the world, one with *this* in it – this story, this object, this idea. You will be helping them, checking on them, refocusing them, encouraging them – but the emphasis is on their work, not yours.

- How will you know what they have learned, and what the next steps should be? This is the plenary when everyone comes back together as a class. The pupils may swap ideas on what has been learned. You may ask them some questions, and they may ask you some questions, too. At the end, you may want to give a final 'assessment' of the whole activity. And you may want to provide a 'teaser' for the next piece of work – a puzzle that remains to be solved, an idea about what happens next, another question that might get the pupils thinking some more. Think like a media producer: at the end of every programme (on the television or online) there will be something about what to do next.

All five stages are important to planning. Many lessons will follow this pattern, but it should not stop you from trying other approaches. The 'initial stimulus' might take up the whole time. Perhaps you have a wonderful, detailed story to tell. That can take up all the time you have. And why not? A wonderful story can last a child a lifetime. Something has been lost in modern schools, since stories have all become ways of starting off lessons, rather than being of value in their own right. RE covers most of the world's best stories, fabulous stories of adventure, of peace, of trials and tribulations, of celebrations. Make use of the fact that the religious stories available to you, today, are those that have – in many cases – been told and retold for hundreds or thousands of years. They are 'classics', every one. Incidentally, the skill of story *telling*, in contrast to story *reading*, is worth practising. Being able to look the pupils in their eyes, while telling a story, can add to the magic. So an 'initial stimulus' might take up the whole lesson, and a 'plenary' might take up the whole time too – with a big discussion of things learned before, or with a test covering the whole year. And the 'core' of the lesson might be all that happens – as the pupils could be carrying on with their projects, rehearsing a role-play of a section of the *Mahabharata*, creating a display about the Jewish-Christian Creation narrative.

Task two: Two questions

This task involves reviewing a lesson – if possible, one of your own lessons, but it can be a review of a lesson you have observed. There are two questions, questions that can be asked of any lesson on any topic in any school in the world.

- What did each pupil in the class learn during the lesson? You might want to focus on half a dozen of the pupils, a range of pupils, but you will eventually need to be able to think about every pupil in the class. It is easy to name the topics covered by the teacher. That is not the same as what the pupil has learned. To understand learning means knowing what the pupil knew or could do *at the start of* the lesson, and how that has *changed* by the end of the lesson. There are clues in what the pupil says early in the lesson, and what that same pupil says towards the end of the lesson. And of course you can ask each pupil what they have learned. (Not what they *know*, because they have not *learned* it if they already knew it at the start of the lesson.) So this seems like an easy question to answer, but it is hard and requires a real researcher's attitude.

- Could the same lesson, with the same learning, have taken place with a group of pupils two or three years younger than these pupils? The answer to the question is either 'yes' or 'no'. Whatever age group you are working with, you can think about the lesson being transposed for younger pupils. If the answer is 'yes', then a follow-up question is, how could the lesson have been changed, so that it still suited the pupils being taught, but would be too challenging for younger pupils. This may not involve changing the whole lesson. Typically, it would involve adding one question or one activity. For example, a lesson for Year 5 in the lead-up to Easter is focusing on the *Last Supper*. Having a meal with your closest friends, before what you think may be a terrible event, is something that could be learned by pupils in Year 2 or Year 3. What would make it less suitable to those younger pupils, but still suitable to Year 5 pupils? Perhaps you could add a focus on this being a typical Jewish Seder during the feast of Pesach (Passover), or you could link it forward to the Eucharist in Christian liturgy.

Planning lessons involves planning for these pupils, not just planning a topic. The two questions in this task should be asked again and again throughout your career as a teacher. They will become automatic: you will be answering them before you even think of the questions.

How is progress planned into a series of RE lessons?

However good a single lesson plan is, it needs to be part of a longer series of lessons. In this way, the pupils will build their learning, rather than just keep going. The Jewish writer Sacks says that we should think of a plural society as 'the home we build together' (Sacks 2007). This is a good model for RE to adopt. The teacher and pupils are building a home, creating a world of knowledge, understanding and skills that all – with all our different beliefs and ways of life – can live in together. Long-term planning in RE is important, therefore. Four elements are given here, and – as with every element of RE in this book – these will need to be developed within the relevant RE syllabus for the school in which you are working.

From an ark to an arc

Primary teachers are likely to be familiar with the narrative of Noah's Ark, important to Jewish, Christian and Muslim traditions. It has been a mainstay of primary RE for many decades, despite being a deeply disturbing and – for many – rather inappropriate account to use with primary pupils, as described in Chapter 2. The account of the Ark is one of divine punishment, the drowning of almost the entire population of the world (people and non-human animals), as a result of their sins. Only Noah and his family, and the animals they fit on the ark, survive. At the end of their voyage, realizing they will survive, a rainbow appears as a mark of the covenant between God and humanity. It is a narrative full of shocking events and the questioning of God's behaviour (and the 're-booting' of the relationship with God), along with the institution of a new legal code (the Noachide laws) to help create a more just society. The Noah's Ark narrative is similar, that is, to what happened in the Holocaust of the Second World War, including the 'trial of God' in death camps (described by Jewish writers), and followed by the founding of the United Nations and the UN Declaration of Human Rights. So Noah's Ark is a tough narrative, albeit one taught in primary schools, all too often, as simply a pretty boating story.

Thinking about this account, including the other themes from this account – more suited to younger pupils – described in Chapter 2, how could you plan a lesson about Noah's Ark suitable for different age groups of pupils? It needs to fit in a bigger picture of the RE to be taught during a year. One year, the RE lessons might be all about personal development (and Noah's Ark might be told as a story of sticking to your views), another year, about the relationship with God (with Noah's Ark illustrating the covenant), another year, about people being given environmental responsibility (by God, in this account and that of the Garden of Eden) (with Noah's Ark describing how people can contribute to environmental sustainability). The big picture of RE, for a whole year, might be described as the arc of the lessons to be taught. So you need to move from an ark to an arc. The big picture, or arc, is sometimes described as an 'elevator pitch' for the set of lessons. That is, if you are stuck in an elevator (a lift) with someone, how will you pitch your ideas for the year in the time it takes for the elevator to go between floors? How would you describe RE for the year, in a single sentence? What are the links between all the elements of RE you will cover? Describing this arc to yourself, you should also be able to describe it to the pupils. It is a great activity for the start of the new school year, and can be used as often as you like – to remind the pupils what the 'big picture' is for RE.

Breadth of heaven

When you are planning RE across a school year, you will need to think about the breadth of coverage. Each syllabus will have its own description of, for example, the range to religious traditions to be covered, or the range of coverage within a single religion. If you are planning in 'topics', such as morality, or celebrations, or what it means to be a person, then there are relatively straightforward ways of ensuring breadth. In any topic, you can compare the beliefs and practices of Christians, Hindus and secular Humanists, for example. If, instead, you are planning for to cover a particular religion such as Christianity for the whole year, you can achieve breadth by planning to work on how Christians in different parts of the world practice their religion, or how Roman Catholics, Anglicans and Russian Orthodox differ in their beliefs. You can also plan, across the year, to use different media to teach RE: you can use stories, artefacts, sacred texts, dramas, music, art, field trips, visits from followers of particular traditions, debates and much more. RE can draw on every subject of the curriculum, as we have tried to show throughout this book.

Some new teachers worry about the breadth of RE, and want to simplify it. That is tempting, as religious and non-religious beliefs and practices are so complex and varied. In Chapter 7, on assessment, we said that the most dangerous word in assessment feedback was 'but'. In RE planning the two most dangerous words are 'all' and 'we' – and this is a reminder for you, as problems with these words have been mentioned earlier in the book. Planning for breadth of coverage in RE is a good way of avoiding 'all' and 'we'. Do all Christians celebrate Christmas in the same way, are all Buddhists pacifists and do all Hindus believe in reincarnation? No. Some Christians believe that Christmas is unbiblical; others – who do celebrate Christmas – celebrate Christmas on a different day to 25 December. The same variety can be found in every tradition. And sociological studies of 'real people' find out, time after time, that people who call themselves Christian, Muslim, Buddhist or atheist may believe and practice a lot of things that contradict their professed beliefs. Planning for breadth in RE means breaking down some of this 'all' language. This is important for your pupils, as they, too, have a range of beliefs and practices – even if every single one of them says they belong to the same religion. That idea brings us to the second dangerous word: 'we'. RE teachers often say 'we' in a way that is uncomfortable (and inaccurate) for many of their pupils. 'We celebrate Christmas, but Hindus celebrate Diwali' is an odd thing to say. Who is 'we'? Is it Christians, the English, the people in this school? It is not true of all Christians, or all English people, or – probably – all the people in this school. The use of the word 'we' by a teacher makes anyone who does not do what 'we' do or believe what 'we' believe feel like an outsider. It is a word that excludes. The word 'we' can usually be replaced by the word 'most', so 'We celebrate Christmas' might be replaced by 'Most Christians celebrate Christmas', or by 'Most people in England, whatever their religion or non-religious beliefs, join in celebrations of Christmas'. Those 'most' sentences (which might be 'some' or 'many' or 'a few' sentences, as appropriate) are more accurate and more inclusive.

Planning for breadth in RE, across a year, can therefore make for more accurate and more inclusive teaching and learning.

CASK-conditioned

Along with planning for breadth in RE, you should also plan for depth. Thinking about concepts, attitudes, skills and knowledge, how will the concepts be 'deepened' in RE? Important RE concepts, such as 'sin', 'sacred', 'ritual' or 'community', are big enough and important enough to be 'learned' in the early years of schooling, and learned again and again, at deeper and deeper levels, throughout the rest of a pupil's time in school – and for the rest of life. This should be part of your planning. Pupils are fond of saying 'we've done this before', if any topic is repeated. What do you reply? 'Yes, we've looked at religious descriptions of God before; this time, we will be investigating some of the puzzles that religious and non-religious people have come up with about God', you might reply. Or, 'Yes, we've looked at some of the puzzles people have come up with about God; this time, we will investigate what it means to believe, or not believe, in God'. An earlier topic of images of God might be deepened by looking at medieval portrayals of God in medieval Christian art and in Muslim calligraphy.

Ways in which RE might become increasingly deep is reflected in religious and non-religious traditions themselves. Festivals are celebrated every year, rituals are repeated anew with every generation. There is a lot of repetition. The film *Groundhog Day* describes how the hero wakes up every day, to find he is reliving the same day. In the film, the hero gradually learns from each previous repeated day, and becomes a better person for what he has learned – eventually escaping from the repeated day. It is said that the writer of the film started thinking about immortality, and how we might behave in, and what we might learn from, a constantly changing world. The idea of a repeated day was the writer's way of capturing that idea. It might have come from the idea of constant reincarnation – in Hindu traditions – that only ends once the 'lessons have been learned' and *Moksha*, the escape from *Samsara*, is achieved. The following task helps you plan for those elements of RE that are, inevitably, repeated year after year, and helps you plan for breadth and depth, too.

Task three: It's Easter again

Making use of the syllabus and planning guidance used by your school, plan for lessons on Easter that will suit the ages and abilities of five different year groups. To remind you of things that we mentioned in Chapter 3, try to ensure that pupils who stay at the school for those five years will not say 'oh, no, we've done that before', or, if they do, you will have a good reply.

You might want to explore

- the 'phenomena' of Easter, the artefacts (crosses, icons, hot crossed buns) and the experiences (such as film of Orthodox Easter celebrations);
- questions such as what 'life out of death' or 'resurrection' might mean to pupils;

- biblical texts, as ways to investigate authoritative accounts of the crucifixion;
- accounts from ten-year-old Catholics, Methodists and Quakers, from different parts of the country, or different parts of the world;
- Handel's *Hallelujah chorus*, making sense of its origins, use today and impact within and beyond the Christian community;
- the possibility of using a guided fantasy based upon the appearance of Jesus to two disciples travelling to Emmaus;
- creating works of art inspired by Easter themes such as 'Back from the Dead' or 'My Hope for the Future' (adapted from Stern 2018a).

Each of these approaches could be taught at a higher or lower level. The idea of planning for a series of five years of lessons is to help you think of longer-term planning, from the point of view of pupils' continuing learning.

How can planning address the whole range of pupil abilities and needs?

For many years, most psychologists thought that intelligence was a matter of 'more' or 'less', and IQ tests were used to measure the overall intelligence of pupils and adults alike. There are many problems with IQ tests, including their cultural biases and the lack of a clear relationship between IQ and anything other than the ability to complete IQ tests. Although IQ is not a reliable guide to intelligence, people still vary in their intelligence, and teachers need to understand – and cater for – the whole range of abilities and needs of their pupils. In recent decades, the approach to abilities and needs has broadened. Special educational needs, disabilities, gifts and talents, having English as an additional language – all these, and more – have been taken account of in schools.

One of the developments in psychological accounts that many teachers found helpful was an account of the breadth – not just the 'quantity' – of intelligence. Since the 1980s, Howard Gardner has been suggesting that there are different *types* of intelligences (Gardner 1993). Although he has his critics, and has more recently criticized his own thinking, acknowledgement of these different intelligences makes demands on the teacher to cater for different learners. (Interestingly, Gardner did not include Spiritual Intelligence in his list.) Whether or not you agree with his ideas, pupils do often show very different types of aptitudes and talents and ways of learning. A wise RE teacher will include many different types of tasks and assessment strategies which appeal to and draw on the different skills and abilities of the students in the class. Think about how the following intelligences might be manifest in the pupils you will teach:

- linguistic,
- musical,

- bodily/kinaesthetic,
- visual/spatial,
- intra-personal,
- interpersonal,
- logical,
- naturalistic.

In long-term planning for RE, you should think of ways in which you can teach that will bring out each of these kinds of intelligence. RE will be much more engaging if there are various uses of language, music, physical engagement and so on. There is a very long history of religious traditions understanding the need to take account of a whole range of abilities in this way. A Christian church service, or a visit to a Gurdwara, will include some talk, some music, some singing, some physical movement, some use of pictures, some social interaction, some time to think and in most cases some food as well. Every sense will be stimulated, every 'type of intelligence' addressed, every level of need at least partly met. This is not the result of religions engaging psychologists in designing their places of worship: it is the result of wanting to include and engage with as many people as possible in the religious tradition. Teachers of primary RE should therefore see the religious traditions themselves as clues to meeting the needs of all their pupils.

There are dangers with making too much use of a theory like that of Gardner. (What dangers can you think of?) Some have responded by adding another type of intelligence: 'spiritual intelligence'. (How would you describe 'spiritual intelligence'?) Cooling et al. (http://www.rethinking.co.uk) list potential abilities and skills that might be characteristic of a spiritual intelligence quotient. How does the following compare with your definition? Using this list, how spiritually intelligent do you think you are? How would the key religious figures fare? How would religions and worldviews seek to develop these qualities? For example, the Buddhist precept about causing no harm would suit the sixth characteristic of the list:

- A capacity to be flexible.
- A high degree of self-awareness.
- A capacity to face and use suffering.
- A capacity to transcend pain.
- Being inspired by vision and values.
- A reluctance to cause unnecessary harm.
- A tendency to see connections.
- A tendency to ask deep questions and seek fundamental answers.
- An ability to work against convention (http://www.rethinking.co.uk).

One of the biggest dangers in any account of intelligence or ability is to think of pupils as having a fixed quantity of the stuff. An interesting experiment was completed in the 1980s by Hartley, a psychologist (Hartley 1986). Hartley was used to carrying out 'objective' IQ tests and other measures of intelligence, in schools. However, he remembered as a teenager that after he failed an English exam (the equivalent of the GCSE), he would do his English work 'pretending' to be a newsreader from the television. By pretending to be the newsreader, and thinking about what *he* would write, Hartley found that his marks got better and better, and he passed the retake of the English exam. So, as an adult, he tried the same with pupils. They all did a set of IQ and other tests that were supposed to be entirely reliable and objective. Afterwards, he would talk to one pupil, and ask who they thought was the cleverest person in the class. The pupil described this person, and Hartley then asked the pupil to pretend they were that clever person. He set another test – and, to his surprise – the pupils who did the second test, while 'imagining' they were clever, got consistently higher marks.

Task four: Imagine

There is a famous song by John Lennon, *Imagine*. In planning primary RE, the teacher's imagination and the imagination of pupils should all be stretched. That is one of the lessons learned from Hartley's research. Make use of this in your planning.

Create a lesson in which you get every pupil to imagine they have abilities or intelligences that they have not yet demonstrated. Religious accounts of miracles are sometimes about people gaining powers they did not think they had (the blind might see, the crippled might walk, the dead might come back to life), but your task is not quite miraculous. For example, ask the pupils to imagine what it would be like to be omniscient (all-knowing), or to be able to cure people just by touching them, or to be able to be calm in the middle of a war.

How can planning for RE help with planning a career in primary education?

The idea of imagination is as important to you as a teacher as it is to the pupils. RE may be just one of the subjects you teach, but imagine how you could make use of your RE skills over a whole career. In the UK, RE has an unusual status. It is a subject that many primary teachers are given a responsibility for very early in their careers. This may be because it is seen by some head teachers as a relatively low-status subject, and so one that can be led by a less-experienced teacher. But you can use this to your advantage. Coordinating a subject is the best way of developing the skills that you will need later in your career – working with other teachers as well as with the pupils, and working with pupils across the school and not just in your own year group. And RE has a range of subject-specific support – more than is available for most other subjects. NATRE (http://www.natre.org.uk) is the subject association for RE, and is well worth joining, with the excellent journal *RE Today* providing more ideas on teaching the subject that any textbook could come up with. If you are interested in a specific aspect of RE, you might also want to apply for a Farmington Fellowship (http://www.farmington.ac.uk). These are available to primary and secondary teachers who want to develop their RE work, and most of the fellowships involve getting a period of, say, twenty days out of school (either a block of time, or a day a week across the year) to work with RE specialists in universities. Culham St Gabriel's Trust (http://www.cstg.org.uk/) is another organization that is committed to supporting high-quality RE, and is both valuable for its own services to the profession and for being a gateway to other services.

Being interested in RE is, in various ways, helpful for a teaching career. It is a subject whose teachers are characterized by determination (in the face of a complex and ever-expanding discipline), flexibility (covering just about all the world's cultures and practices), the ability to deal with controversy (as everything in RE is controversial, and many of the world's most intractable problems are related to religion), courage (teaching a subject that some think is unimportant and others think is too important to be left to teachers) and much more.

Task five: A retirement speech (already!)

Imagine you are retiring as a teacher. In your career, you will have done many things, but throughout that time, you have kept up your interest in RE. Write a retirement speech – a speech you will give to colleagues and current and former pupils. What will you want to say about your career in teaching, and especially about your interest in RE?

When you have written the speech, put it away somewhere safe. Then, when you really do retire, you can look at it again, and see how good a speech it was!

What is the future of RE?

Early in this book, we described some of the history of RE, and some of the current policies and practices. Having got to the end of the book, it is worth considering the future of the subject. Perhaps in the future it will become part of the National Curriculum, or perhaps the National Curriculum will have less and less influence and other subjects will become more like RE – determined at a local level, and very varied. Some think that the name 'RE' might change, or that the subject will disappear into other subjects – such as humanities or personal and social education. Studying RE around the world (as described in chapter 4 of Stern 2018a), the one thing that can be said with certainty is that the future is uncertain. RE is taught in most countries in the world, but it has a very different structure in each country. (Even the countries of the UK have different approaches to RE.) Half a century ago, sociologists were saying that religion – not RE, but religion itself – was disappearing. Now, though, those sociologists are busy eating their words. Religion is still here, and there are still conflicts within and between religions and between religious and non-religious approaches to life. RE is a 'lively' subject, and all the better for it.

For all the policies and regulations and inspections, school subjects are most influenced by the people doing them – the teachers and their pupils. So the final task of this book asks you to create your own future for RE. 'Be the change you wish to see in the world' is a well-used quotation (attributed to Arleen Lorrance, and also to Gandhi, for which see https://quoteinvestigator.com/2017/10/23/be-change/). What change will you be?

At the start of this book we included some initial comments by student teachers as they began to think about teaching RE. They expressed some misgivings and issues with the subject. Look at what the following student teachers wrote after learning how to teach the subject:

Julia chose the image of George Frederic Watts' *Hope*, from 1886 (http://www.tate.org.uk/art/artworks/watts-hope-n01640):

> I write this at a time when we have just witnessed horrific atrocities committed against innocent children and families attending a concert in Manchester. Every day somewhere in the world, senseless acts of terror are committed in the name of religion. Yet every time I walk into a classroom and talk to the children, I am filled with hope. Hope for a better world; one that respects the planet and all living things. I see the teaching of RE as a significant part of that journey.
>
> Let us hope for a world where people of all faiths and denominations can live side by side in peace.

Elizabeth chose Kandinsky's *Colour Study: Squares with Concentric Circles* of 1913 (http://www.wassilykandinsky.net/work-370.php).

> I have used Kandinsky's Concentric Circles as a metaphor for a multicultural society.
>
> I have found the way in which RE is now to taught, contextualised to the children's experience, to be the most positive way in which we can hope to support younger generations to live in a harmonious multicultural society. By 'learning about' and 'learning from' religion, children are able to appreciate the similarities between cultures, and understand and respect the differences. For those children who are not religious it enables them to see the links between the way religion has influenced their society and their own social, moral, spiritual and cultural development. I feel a lot more confident in my ability to teach RE successfully, and to deal with difficult situations that arise in multicultural classrooms. I now feel confident that I could link RE successfully with PSHE lessons to enhance the learning in both areas and that links with Art could provide additional opportunities for reflection and expression. I fully appreciate the significance of RE to the future well-being of children and our society as a whole.

Figure 8.2 Stained glass window, Notre Dame, Paris

Catherine took this photograph of the beautiful window in Notre Dame Cathedral, Paris (Figure 8.2). At the start of her ITT course, she felt positive about RE but asked 'How am I going to explain this beautiful concept of religion and faith that is so delicate and can change and look so different when you start to unpick and examine it ??'

Later in the year she chose another colourful and stunning image (viewable at https://trex209.deviantart.com/art/Colorful-Shapes-159948961) and wrote the following:

> This picture is not by a particularly well known or by famous artist – it is something beautiful and colourful but seemingly possible to create one's self (if you had skill enough with a computer perhaps). It is contemporary. It is not something sacrosanct, sacred, holy and foreign which needs to be only looked upon with reverence. Religion is something of today for this world, not another. Religion is not something that has to be left on the wall, admired only from afar. It is something that can and should be picked up and handled. That is to be interacted with. …The picture is wondrous and bright, colourful, and bold and I hope that the colour and brightness that religion can bring will be seen through my teaching.
>
> The picture is more ordered – the shapes are more regular and defined, a sign that my understanding of the subject is more ordered, as is the information I have about the subject and religion. The forms are delineated and more uniform as I know the aims and structures that govern the subject. …The colours and technique used here still seem to allow light to come through – as if the picture is glowing a little. There is a certain transparency to the picture – it makes me think that you could hold it up to the light, and similar to the stained glass, you could look through and see things through a different colour filter. It would change your perspective, could change the way you see things.

Did you write something and choose an image about your relationship with RE after reading the first chapter? If you did you might like to find a second image and consider if and how your thinking has changed, possibly through reading this and other texts and as you practice teaching in the classroom.

Task six: Be the change

Plan the future of RE. What would you like RE to be in primary schools in the future. If you were able to plan it, what would be in the subject, how would it be taught, how would it fit with other subjects. The future might involve changing the subject radically, or even abolishing the subject – but even so, how would you plan for a curriculum without RE, where would all the life-and-death issues currently covered by RE be taught and where would mystery and the meaning of life be addressed? If you think – as we think – that the subject should survive and thrive, what will it be like?

  This is your chance to be the change. The authors of this book were both schoolteachers, and both taught RE (along with other subjects). Somehow, we both ended up training teachers and writing about RE and influencing the subject. So it really can come true. Now, be the change you hope to see!

Summary

This chapter centred on planning, as a way of dealing with the flood of practical issues facing teachers of RE. With good planning, teachers can deal with the inevitable surprises that come their way, and they can remain focused on how all pupils progress in the subject. Teachers make the future: they are educating the next generation. Planning in RE can also mean planning for the future of the subject, as RE is one of the most changeable subjects of the curriculum. Rather than getting overwhelmed by practical issues, teachers of RE can contribute to the practice of RE teaching itself.

Recommended reading

Wintersgill, B (ed) (2017) *Big Ideas for Religious Education*; Exeter: University of Exeter.

Bibliography

Books

Ashton, E (2000) *Religious Education in the Early Years*; Abingdon, Oxfordshire: Routledge.

One of the few books (along with Lowndes 2012) specializing in early years RE.

Barnes, L P (ed) (2012) *Debates in Religious Education*; London: Routledge.

For those wanting to dig deeper into the key issues in RE, this (along with Broadbent and Brown 2002, below) is a helpful and wide-ranging textbook.

Barnes, L P (ed) (2017) *Learning to Teach Religious Education in the Secondary School: A Companion to School Experience – Third Edition*; Abingdon, Oxfordshire: Routledge.

One of the standard textbooks for those training to teach RE in secondary schools, this is particularly helpful for Key Stage 2 teachers wishing to stretch their pupils – and to know what will be happening next.

Broadbent, L and Brown, A (eds) (2002) *Issues in Religious Education*; London: RoutledgeFalmer.

For those wanting to dig deeper into the key issues in RE, this (along with Barnes 2012, above) is a helpful and wide-ranging textbook.

Erricker, C, Lowndes, J and Bellchambers, E (2011) *Primary Religious Education – A New Approach: Conceptual Enquiry in Primary RE*; London: Routledge.

This book takes a conceptual enquiry approach, used in several Agreed Syllabi. It is useful for the historical context of the subject, and there are useful case studies throughout to link the theory with practice.

Grimmitt, M (ed) (2000) *Pedagogies of Religious Education*; Great Wakering, Essex: McCrimmon.

For those wanting to know about how RE developed its various approaches, this is an excellent book, written by many of the leading researchers and contributors to debates on UK RE.

Hull, J M (1998) *Utopian Whispers: Moral, Religious and Spiritual Values in Schools*; Norwich: RMEP.

A fascinating account by one of the world's most influential figures in RE.

Lowndes, J (2012) *The Complete Multifaith Resource for Primary Religious Education: Ages 4–7*; Abingdon, Oxfordshire: Rout.

A reliable guide for younger children.

McCreery, E, Palmer, S and Voiels, V (2008) *Teaching Religious Education: Primary and Early Years*; Exeter: Learning Matters.

It includes practical and reflective tasks and the case studies are helpful in linking theory with practice and giving further ideas of how to teach for effective learning in RE.

Pett, S (ed) (2015) *Religious Education: The Teacher's Guide*; Birmingham: RE Today Services.

The three main sections relate to effective subject leadership in RE, how RE can promote pupils' learning and development and a concluding section on what teachers will need to know about the six principal world religions and non-religious worldviews. It offers a wealth of ideas for the teacher of RE and focuses on the key information that all RE teachers need to know to teach effectively.

Rivett, R (ed) (2007) *A Teacher's Handbook of Religious Education: Third Edition*; Birmingham: RE Today Services.

Like Pett's book, this is a very clear professional guide.

Stern, L J (2018a) *Teaching Religious Education: Researchers in the Classroom – Second Edition*; London: Bloomsbury.

A guide to RE teaching across primary and secondary age-groups, based around research tasks that pupils and teachers alike can carry out. An investigative approach to RE, with guidance on RE around the world.

Teece, G (2012) *The Primary Teacher's Guide to Religious Education*; Oxford: Scholastic, Oxford.

A very practical book with helpful subject knowledge guidance on the six religions most often taught in RE, and plenty of teaching tips too.

Watson, B and Thompson, P (2006) *The Effective Teaching of Religious Education: Second Edition*; London: Routledge.

This book provides a chance for the teacher to really consider how to integrate theory with practice and encourages debate about some of the issues associated with the subject of RE. There are some very thoughtful and innovative ideas and strategies outlined within its pages for effective and dynamic RE.

Webster, M (2010) *Creative Approaches to Teaching Primary RE*; Harlow, Essex: Pearson.

One of the best creative textbooks on RE.

Wintersgill, B (ed) (2017) *Big Ideas for Religious Education*; Exeter: University of Exeter.

An interesting guide to what UK RE is all about, providing a useful framework for understanding what all RE teachers (and pupils) are likely to need to know about.

Websites

Association of RE Inspectors, Advisors and Consultants (AREIAC) (http://www.areiac.org.uk)

AREIAC offers some great support for all teachers of RE and gives you a link to the wider RE community.

RE Online (http://www.reonline.org.uk)

An excellent collection of all things RE.

RE Today (http://www.retoday.org.uk) and the National Association of Teachers of RE (NATRE) (http://www.natre.org.uk) (@NATREupdate)

This is the main supplier of RE resources and support in England and Wales.

References

Ahlberg, A (1991 [1989]) *Heard It in the Playground*; London: Puffin.

Alexander, R J (2004) *Towards Dialogic Teaching: Rethinking Classroom Talk*; Thirsk: Dialogos.

Alexander, R J (2006) *Education as Dialogue: Moral and Pedagogical Choices for a Runaway World*; Thirsk: Hong Kong Institute of Education with Dialogos.

Alexander, R J (2009) *Towards a New Primary Curriculum: A Report from the Cambridge Primary Review. Part 2: The Future*; Cambridge: University of Cambridge, Faculty of Education.

All-Party Parliamentary Group on Religious Education [APPGRE] (2013) *RE: The Truth Unmasked – The Supply of and Support for Religious Education Teachers*; London: The All-Party Parliamentary Group on Religious Education.

Aristotle (1984) *The Complete Works of Aristotle*; Princeton, New Jersey: Princeton University Press.

Armstrong, K (1993) *A History of God: From Abraham to the Present – The 4000-Year Quest for God*; London: Vintage.

Avest, I ter, Jozsa, D-P, Knauth, T, Rosón, J and Skeie, G (eds) (2009) *Dialogue and Conflict on Religion: Studies of Classroom Interaction in European Countries*; Münster: Waxmann.

Bakhtin, M M (1986) *Speech Genres and Other Late Essays: Edited by Caryl Emerson and Michael Holquist*; Austin, Texas: University of Texas Press.

Bastide, D (1987) *Religious Education 5–12*; London: Falmer Press.

Benjamin, S (2002) *The Micropolitics of Inclusive Education: An Ethnography*; Buckingham: Open University Press.

Black, P and Wiliam, D (1998) 'Inside the Black Box: Raising Standards through Classroom Assessment', *Phi Delta Kappan*, 89:2, pp 139–48.

Blaylock, L (ed) (2001) *Listening to Children in Primary Religious Education*; Birmingham: PCfRE.

Blaylock, L (ed) (2004) *Representing Religions*; Birmingham: Christian Education.

Bloom, B S (ed) (1965) *The Taxonomy of Educational Objectives. Book 1: Cognitive Domain*; London: Longman.

Bloom, B S, Krathwohl, D R and Masia, B B (1965) *The Taxonomy of Educational Objectives. Book 2: Affective Domain*; London: Longman.

Broadbent, L and Brown, A (eds) (2002) *Issues in Religious Education*; London: RoutledgeFalmer.

Bruner, J (1977) *The Process of Education*; Cambridge, Massachusetts: Harvard University Press.

Buber, M (2002 [1965]) *Between Man and Man*; London: Routledge.

Carrington, B and Troyna, B (eds) (1988) *Children and Controversial Issues: Strategies for the Early and Middle Years of Schooling*; London: Falmer.

Carroll, L (1998 [1865, 1872]) *Alice's Adventures in Wonderland* and *Through the Looking Glass*; London: Penguin.

Cavalletti, S (1992) *Religious Potential of the Child: Experiencing Scripture and Liturgy with Young Children*; Chicago: Liturgy Training Publications.

Chödzin, S and Kohn, A (illustrations by Marie Cameron) (1997) *The Barefoot Book of Buddhist Tales* [also published as *The Wisdom of the Crows and Other Stories*]; Bath: Barefoot Books.

Clarke, C and Woodhead, L (2015) *A New Settlement: Religion and Belief in Schools*; London: Westminster Faith Debates (also available online at http://www.faithdebates.org.uk).

Clarke, C and Woodhead, L (2018) *A New Settlement Revised: Religion and Belief in Schools*; London: Westminster Faith Debates (also available online at http://www.faithdebates.org.uk).

Commission on RE (2018) *Final Report: Religion and Worldviews: The Way Forward – A National Plan for RE*; London: Religious Education Council of England and Wales.

Cooling, M (2009) *Christianity through Art: A Resource for Teaching Religious Education through Art*; Norwich: RMEP.

Cooling, T (1994) *Concept Cracking: Exploring Christian Beliefs in School*; Stapleford, Nottinghamshire: The Stapleford Centre (also available online at http://www.stapleford-centre.org/).

Cooling, T and Cooling, M (2004) *Concept Cracking: A Practical Way to Teach Big Ideas in RE*; Nottingham: The Stapleford Centre.

Copley, T (2005) *Indoctrination, Education and God: The Struggle for the Mind*; London: SPCK.

Dalton, J and Smith, D (1987) *Extending Children's Special Abilities: Strategies for Primary Classrooms*; Melbourne, Australia: Ministry of Education.

Department of Education and Science (DES) (1988) *Education Reform Act*; London: HMSO.

Department for Education (DfE) (2013) *The National Curriculum in England: Framework Document – December 2014*; London: Department for Education.

Desailly, J (2015) *Creativity in the Primary Classroom: Second Edition*; London: SAGE.

Donaldson, J and Scheffler, A (2008) *Stick Man*; London: Alison Green Books.

Durka, G (2002) *The Teacher's Calling: A Spirituality for Those Who Teach*; New York: Paulist Press.

Dweck, C S (2006) *Mindset: The New Psychology of Success*; New York: Ballantine Books.

Ehlert, L (2005) *Leaf Man*; Orlando, Florida: Harcourt.

Einstein, A (1955) 'Old Man's Advice to Youth: "Never Lose a Holy Curiosity"', *LIFE Magazine*, 2 May, p 64.

Erricker, C, Lowndes, J and Bellchambers, E (2011) *Primary Religious Education – A New Approach: Conceptual Enquiry in Primary RE*; London: Routledge.

Ewens, A and Stone, M (2001) *Teaching about God, Worship and Spirituality: Practical Approaches for 7–11 Year Olds*; Norwich: RMEP.

Fageant, J and Blaylock, L (eds) (1998) *Faith in the Future: An Anthology of Pupils' Writing from the National RE Festival Questionnaire*; Birmingham: PCfRE.

Fines, J and Nichol, J (1997) *Teaching Primary History*; Oxford: Heinemann

Freathy, G, Freathy, R, Doney, J, Walshe, K and Teece, G (2015) *The RE-Searchers: A New Approach to Religious Education in Primary Schools*; Exeter: University of Exeter.

Freire, P (1970 [1968], 1993) *Pedagogy of the Oppressed*; Harmondsworth: Penguin.

Fromm, E (2013 [1967]) *Psychoanalysis and Religion*; New York: Open Road.

Gaarder, J (1994) *Sophie's World*; London: Phoenix.

Gardner, H (1993) *Multiple Intelligences: The Theory in Practice*; New York: Basic Books.

Grimmitt, M (1987) *Religious Education and Human Development*; Great Wakering, Essex: McCrimmon.

Grimmitt, M, Grove, J, Hull, J M and Spencer, L (1991) *A Gift to the Child: Religious Education in the Primary School*; London: Simon & Schuster.

Hartley, R (1986) 'Imagine You're Clever', *Journal of Child Psychology and Psychiatry*, 27:3, pp 383–98.

Hartman, B and Nagy, K K (2008) *The Lion Storyteller Bible*; Oxford: Lion.

Hatfield, E (2004) *Feeling Included? A Critical Analysis of the Impact of Pedagogy on Inclusion in a Primary School*; Hull: Unpublished MA Dissertation, University of Hull.

Hay, D (2007) *Why Spirituality Is Difficult for Westerners*; Exeter: Societas Essays in Political & Cultural Criticism.

Hay, D with Nye, R (2006) *The Spirit of the Child: Revised Edition*; London: Jessica Kingsley.

Hayward, M (2007) *Christianity in Religious Education at Key Stage 3*; Coventry: University of Warwick.

Holland, J (1997) *Coping with Bereavement: A Handbook for Teachers*; Cardiff: Cardiff Academic Press.

Holland, J (2016) *Responding to Loss and Bereavement in Schools: A Training Resource to Assess, Evaluate and Improve the School Response*; London: Jessica Kingsley.

Honoré, C (2004) *In Praise of Slow: How a Worldwide Movement Is Challenging the Cult of Speed*; London: Orion.

Hull, J M (1991) *God-Talk with Young Children: Notes for Parents and Teachers*; London: Continuum.

Hull, J M (2013) *The Tactile Heart: Blindness and Faith*; London: SCM Press.

Hunt, A E and Jonke, T (2001) *The Tale of Three Trees*; Oxford: Lion.

Inkpen, M (1995) *Nothing*; London: Hodder & Stoughton.

Kincheloe, J L (2008) *Critical Pedagogy Primer: Second Edition*; New York: Peter Lang.

Lawrence-Lightfoot, S (2003) *The Essential Conversation: What Parents and Teachers Can Learn from Each Other*; New York: Ballantine.

Lewis, C S (2000) *The Complete Chronicles of Narnia*; London: HarperCollins.

Liedgren, P (2018) 'Minorities with Different Values at School – The Case of Jehovah's Witnesses', *British Journal of Religious Education*, 40:1, pp 31–43.

Logan, J (1998) *Artefacts for an Occasion*; Isleworth: BFSS National RE Centre, Brunel University.

Martins, I M and Matoso, M (2010) *When I Was Born*; London: Tate.

McCreery, E, Palmer, S and Voiels, V (2008) *Teaching Religious Education: Primary and Early Years*; Exeter: Learning Matters.

McKee, D (1980) *Not Now, Bernard*; London: Red Fox.

Moustakas, C and Moustakas, K (2004) *Loneliness, Creativity & Love: Awakening Meanings in Life*; Bloomington, Indiana: Xlibris.

Ng, Y-L (2012) 'Spiritual Development in the Classroom: Pupils' and Educators' Learning Reflections', *International Journal of Children's Spirituality*, 17:2, pp 167–85.

Office for Standards in Education (Ofsted) (2004) *Promoting and Evaluating Pupils' Spiritual, Moral, Social and Cultural Development*; London: Stationery Office.

Office for Standards in Education (Ofsted) (2010) *Transforming Religious Education: Religious Education in Schools 2006–09*; Manchester: Ofsted.

Office for Standards in Education (Ofsted) (2013) *Religious Education: Realising the Potential*; Manchester: Ofsted.

Office for Standards in Education (Ofsted) (2016) *School Inspection Handbook: Handbook for Inspecting Schools in England under Section 5 of the Education Act 2005*; Manchester: Ofsted.

Olson, C (ed) (2005) *Original Buddhist Sources: A Reader*; New Brunswick, New Jersey: Rutgers University Press.

Otto, R (1958 [1950]) *The Idea of the Holy: Second Edition*; Oxford: Oxford University Press.

Palmer, J A (ed) (2001) *Fifty Modern Thinkers on Education: From Piaget to the Present Day*; London: Routledge.

Payne, P G and Wattchow, B (2009) 'Phenomenological Deconstruction, Slow Pedagogy and the Corporeal Turn in Wild Environmental/Outdoor Education', *Canadian Journal of Environmental Education*, 14, pp 15–32.

Pett, S (ed) (2015) *Religious Education: The Teacher's Guide*; Birmingham: RE Today Services.

Pickering, S (ed) (2017) *Teaching Outdoors Creatively*; Abingdon, Oxfordshire: Routledge.

Pound, L (2009) *How Children Learn 3: Contemporary Thinking and Theorists*; London: Practical Pre-School Books.

Priestley, J (1997) 'Spirituality, Curriculum and Education', *International Journal of Children's Spirituality*, 2:1, pp 23–34.

Prothero, S (2007) *Religious Literacy: What Every American Needs to Know – And Doesn't*; New York: HarperCollins.

Qualifications and Curriculum Authority (QCA) (2004) *Religious Education: The Non-Statutory National Framework*; London: QCA.

Religious Education Council of England and Wales (REC) (2013a) *A Review of Religious Education in England*; London: The Religious Education Council of England and Wales.

Religious Education Council of England and Wales (REC) (2013b) *A Curriculum Framework for Religious Education in England*; London: The Religious Education Council of England and Wales.

Revell, L and Walters, R (2010) *Christian Student RE Teachers, Objectivity and Professionalism*; Canterbury: CLIENT.

Rumi (1995) *The Essential Rumi*; Harmondsworth: Penguin.

de Rynck, P (2009) *Understanding Paintings: Bible Stories and Classical Myths in Art*; London: Thames and Hudson.

Sacks, J (2007) *The Home We Build Together: Recreating Society*; London: Continuum.

Seaman, A and Owen, G (2012) *Teaching Christianity at Key Stage 1*; London: Church House Publishing.

School Curriculum and Assessment Authority (SCAA) (1994a) *Model Syllabuses for Religious Education. Model 1: Living Faiths Today*; London: SCAA.

School Curriculum and Assessment Authority (SCAA) (1994b) *Model Syllabuses for Religious Education. Model 2: Questions and Teachings*; London: SCAA.

Smart, N (1973) *The Phenomenon of Religion*; London: Macmillan.

Stern, L J (1995) *Learning to Teach: A Guide for School-Based Initial and In-Service Training*; London: David Fulton.

Stern, L J (2003) *Involving Parents*; London: Continuum.

Stern, L J (2006) *Teaching Religious Education: Researchers in the Classroom*; London: Continuum.

Stern, L J (2007) *Schools and Religions: Imagining the Real*; London: Continuum.

Stern, L J (2009) *The Spirit of the School*; London: Continuum.

Stern, L J (2018a) *Teaching Religious Education: Researchers in the Classroom – Second Edition*; London: Bloomsbury.

Stern, L J (2018b) 'Curiosity Killed the SAT: The Role of Research in Redirecting Performativity in Initial Teacher Education', *Research in Education*, 100:1, pp 50–64.

Stern, L J and Backhouse, A (2011) 'Dialogic Feedback for Children and Teachers: Evaluating the "Spirit of Assessment"', *International Journal of Children's Spirituality*, 16:4, pp 331–46.

Stern, L J and Shillitoe, R (2018) *Evaluation of Prayer Spaces in Schools: The Contribution of Prayer Spaces to Spiritual Development*; York: York St John University (also available online at https://ray.yorksj.ac.uk/id/eprint/3103/ and at https://www.prayerspacesinschools.com/research2017).

Stickney, D (1997) *Water Bugs and Dragonflies: Explaining Death to Young Children*; Cleveland, Ohio: Pilgrim Press.

Stone, M and Brennan, J (2009) *'See' RE Stories from Christianity: Guided Visualisations for Children Aged 7–11*; Norwich: RMEP.

Stone, M K (1995) *Don't Just Do Something – Sit There: Developing Children's Spiritual Awareness*; Norwich: RMEP.

Teece, G (2001) *The Primary Teacher's Guide to Religious Education*; Leamington Spa: Scholastic.

Tomlinson, J and Howard, P (2002) *The Owl Who Was Afraid of the Dark*; London: Egmont.

Vaisey, G and Gwillym, L (2004) *A Wet and Windy Harvest for Puddles*; Blakeney, Gloucestershire: Books@Press.

Varley, S (1984) *Badger's Parting Gifts*; London: Andersen Press.

Watson, B and Thompson, P (2006) *The Effective Teaching of Religious Education: Second Edition*; London: Routledge.

Weston, D (2003) 'Children Talking Online', *RE Today*, 21:1, pp 30–1.

Wiliam, D (2005) *Formative Assessment: The Research Evidence*; Educational Testing Service (also available online at http://www.ets.org/).

Williams, M (2007 [1922]) *The Velveteen Rabbit: Or How Toys Become Real*; London: Egmont.

Wintersgill, B (ed) (2017) *Big Ideas for Religious Education*; Exeter: University of Exeter.

Index